Morning
in my Heart

Morning in my Heart

H. G. Mackay

WITH HELEN H. MACKAY

GOSPEL FOLIO PRESS
P. O. Box 2041, Grand Rapids MI 49501-2041

Cover design by J. B. Nicholson, Jr.

Published by Gospel Folio Press
P. O. Box 2041, Grand Rapids, MI 49501-2041

ISBN 1-882701-04-6

Printed in the United States of America

Dedication

If the refining fire of the Judgment Seat of Christ leaves any residue of my life and service, all glory and praise will belong to my faithful High Priest, the Lord Jesus Christ, whose intercessory ministry has sustained me at all times. And surely much credit, on the human side, will be due to my supportive wife, Gertrude Marjory Eckert Mackay, who has been at my side for sixty years, amid all the circumstances of life, sharing fully in its joys and sorrows, its trials and triumphs.

Contents

Foreword

"My history professor says the three greatest influences on the twentieth century were Darwin, Marx, and Freud." I was the speaker, pontificating from the height of my college freshman superiority.

"No wonder the world is in such a mess!" The reply boomed from the tall man with deep-set green eyes that seemed to bore through me, until I also caught the faint hint of a kindly twinkle somewhere in their depths. We were seated across the Mackay family dining table from each other. I had been no stranger to that table since enrolling in the University of North Carolina at Greensboro, then called Woman's College, the previous September. Stan, the Mackays' second son, and I had met in August at the Bristol Bible Conference and had been dating steadily ever since.

To a freshman, away from home for the first time, bombarded daily with intellectually and spiritually unsettling ideas, Harold Mackay was an enigma: he was a flint from whom I sometimes stubbornly tried to elicit a spark, as in this conversation; but he was also a comforting boundary marker, also evident in this exchange. I discovered that even though he had not attended college, he was one of the best-read men I had ever met. One evening, when I brought up some ideas of the philosopher-psychologist William James, he immediately expanded on them—and then showed me their flaws.

Harold G. Mackay ("Dad," as he asked me to call him just after performing the wedding ceremony that made me Mrs. Stanley R. Mackay) was my father-in-law for nearly thirty-three years. His Lord took him home to heaven this April (1993). Shortly before Dad's death, his oldest son Jack discovered a manuscript among his papers. None of us knew that he had begun, in his eighties, to write this account of his life and Christian service. Toward the end of writing it, he evidently decided not to publish it. It seems to have been more a spiritual exercise, a recalling of the path in which the Lord had led him for over sixty years. As friends in the Greensboro assembly and elsewhere heard of this, they urged us to publish it. This was not feasible in its current condition, however, for a number of reasons: it sometimes lacked transitions, it occasionally needed some added details, and its organizational pattern had changed after Chapter 8, leading to some loss of continuity.

Soon Jack turned up another manuscript, this one a history of the Greensboro assembly. The more incomplete chapters in the autobiography had been those dealing with Greensboro; now we could see why. Having already dealt with the assembly in some detail, he felt no need to repeat much of the same information in the biography. Ron, the youngest son, later discovered a missing chapter of the autobiography among some papers he had borrowed to get information for a videotape he had compiled as a sixtieth wedding anniversary memento for Mom and Dad.

We also had access to sixty years of daily diary entries, as well as Dad's other records: a journal of his developing health conditions, a log detailing steps in his convalescence after the ensuing brain surgery, travel logs, a record of dates of significant family events. We thus had the material to fill out the manuscript where this was needed. My position as a family member furnished me with some insights into Dad's thinking; my position as a member of the English department of a local four-year liberal arts college meant that I have had to develop some of the practical skills of revising and editing that would enable me to undertake this task. It has been a particular joy for me to be able to do so. The result is a labor of love and a tribute to one of the Lord's special servants.

My guiding principles have been to preserve Dad's own words insofar as possible and try to keep additions and alterations as consistent as I could with his style. Chapters 9-12 are a new arrangement of his later chapters in the original manuscript. I did this by piecing together passages from the assembly history with passages from the autobiography. Where I added an occasional detail not found in either of these sources, it came from his diaries and logs, or sometimes from my mother-in-law's recollections.

If there are errors or inconsistencies in this narrative, they are mine, not Dad's. At times it was difficult to determine the exact connection between one piece of information and another. For most such puzzlements, Mom was a good source of clarification; at other times I have had to take small leaps of faith which I hope will nevertheless keep the account accurate.

My one original contribution to this book is its title. Dad's own title was "Recollections of the Goodness and Guidance of the Lord," which seemed rather long. *Morning in My Heart* is taken from the theme song which introduced his long-running Greensboro radio program *Your Bible Says*. The song, "It Is Morning in My Heart," speaks of the joy of salvation and the Christian life. Since Dad chose that song and kept it as his theme song for so many years, it surely addressed a deep wellspring of significance in his own heart. Mornings can sometimes be dark, and he faced many trials in his life, particularly the brain surgery which is the subject of Chapter 11. Nevertheless, to Dad, it was always "morning," a new beginning, a new day to perform some service for his Lord.

For any readers who are unfamiliar with assembly principles, it may be useful to add a brief explanation of Dad's beliefs about the recognition and financial support of those engaged in full-time service for the Lord. Otherwise, some of the incidents and points in this book may be unclear. These are principles by which my father-in-law lived and which shaped his thinking and actions.

First, full-time workers are not selected or ordained by any human institution or individual. They are called by God, they begin to use the spiritual gifts He has given them, and if this service shows by its results ("fruit") that it is indeed divinely-commissioned, any assembly who so desires may choose to "commend" them. The letter of commendation is neither a contract nor a promise of financial support. It is simply a practical reassurance to others that the commending body of believers see this person as called of God and sound in doctrine and life.

Second, such workers depend completely on the Lord to meet their financial needs. They have no promise of monetary support, even from an assembly among whom they live and minister, nor would they accept such a promise if offered. When Christ sent out the seventy disciples to minister, He told them they were free to partake of what was given to them in the places they went, "for the laborer is worthy of his hire" (Lk. 10:7). According to this principle, the assembly may, indeed *should,* give to meet the practical needs of those who serve, but such gifts are as the Lord leads and provides, not according to a predetermined contractual decision.

Third, the full-time worker is not referred to as "Reverend," a title used in Scripture only for God, nor is he considered *the* pastor or minister, although pastoral work, preaching, teaching, and other forms of service are all part of his labor for the Lord. He labors to see a body of elders raised up to care for such local gatherings.

In revising and editing *Morning in My Heart,* I have profited greatly by the encouragement and assistance of others. I want to thank especially my longsuffering husband, Stan, who has been repeatedly interrupted from his own work by my pleas to "listen to this paragraph and tell me what you think." I owe a debt of gratitude to C. R. (Dick) Andrews for reading and commenting on chapters related to Dad's work in Greensboro. I have also been very dependent on my dear mother-in-law, Mrs. Gertrude Mackay, for clarification, identification of people and places, and anecdotes. J. B. Nicholson, Jr. has helped at each stage of editing, and he is also overseeing the publication of the book. Barry Snyder, of the Greensboro assembly, provided the initial stimulus and encouragement that caused us to consider publishing Dad's autobiography. And there have been many who have contributed information, pictures, and often happy memories of past years. To each I offer special thanks and prayers for the Lord's blessing.

Helen H. Mackay
June, 1993

Preface

"Only one life, 'twill soon be past, Only what's done for Christ will last." In the early decades of the twentieth century, these words were often heard in Christian circles, printed in Christian literature, and emblazoned on plaques hung on the walls of many Christian homes. And they burned their way into my newly-softened heart.

My life had experienced a dramatic change in 1926. The One who was to become the Captain of my salvation had called, and the direction of my life had been diametrically altered. But how was I going to live my new life? That's where the little couplet quoted above exerted such an influence on me. There could be only one wise decision: the one and only earthly life I would ever have must be lived wholeheartedly for Christ and for Him alone.

The day after I definitely made this decision to invest my time and energies in the service of the Lord, I went to a prayer meeting in the evening. After the service, a Christian businessman drew me aside and said, "Harold, I would like to have you become the travelling representative for my company." He was president and owner of a flourishing enterprise in my home city of Galt. "It will be an opportunity for you to make a lot of money, but it will be a challenge to your Christian testimony."

I thanked him, but told him of my decision to devote my life to service for Christ. Warmly grasping my hand, he exclaimed, "God bless you, my dear young brother! You're going to represent a much greater company than mine—the Company of God the Father, God the Son, and God the Holy Spirit. Here, take this as a little share in your work for the Lord." And he placed in my hand a roll of bills—the first of many thousands of such unsolicited gifts I have received during these sixty years of dependence upon the Lord for my support in His work.

A Sunday School class of boys, open-air meetings, tent meetings, children's services, youth gatherings, gospel campaigns, Bible-teaching meetings, children's camps, summer conferences, holiday Bible conferences, Bible school classes, baccalaureate sermons, shop meetings, radio broadcasts, telecasts, civic functions, weddings, funerals, cruise ship chapel services, rescue missions—what a variety of opportunities God has given during these sixty years to minister His Word and to proclaim the "old, old story of Jesus and His love." I have had the privilege of working directly with choice servants of the Lord, and I have had the equal privilege of following behind and supporting others. Shortly after moving to Greensboro, I wrote to my father, an experienced elder of many years:

"I feel like one of Solomon's stonesquarers (1 Ki. 5:18). Brother [Lester] Wilson has been down in the quarry, and has brought up some splendid building material in the form of soundly-converted men and women. Now the Head of the Church has entrusted to me the sacred task of preparing them to fit into His building, the local assembly. It is arduous labor, but most rewarding."

I have been prompted to record the following recollections by the exhortation in Deuteronomy 8:2: "Thou shalt remember all the way which the Lord thy God hath led thee . . . to humble thee . . . to prove thee . . . to know what was in thine heart, whether thou wouldest keep His commandments or no." Writing them has been a humbling experience, with its constant reminder of my failings; and yet, against this backdrop of human weakness, there has been the equally-constant revelation of the unfailing faithfulness of the Heavenly Master it has been my honored privilege to serve. I have rejoiced again at the wonder of His gracious guidance amid the increasing perplexities of life. I can only say with the prophet Zephaniah, "He faileth not" (3:5).

Harold G. Mackay
1990

1
Birth and Boyhood

"With an ancestry like yours, if you'll stay out of the path of big trucks, you should live to be an old man." The speaker was an internationally-known neurosurgeon who had removed an acoustical tumor from under my skull, a tumor he described as "large as a tennis ball and as hard as a rock." He had inquired about my ancestors and other pertinent matters as he gave me final instructions before releasing me from the Bowman Gray School of Medicine in Winston Salem, North Carolina, where the surgery had been performed.

His reference was to my grandparents who came from the highlands of northern Scotland, where the Mackays were a large and influential clan. His prediction proved correct, as I am now in my 80's, although I prefer to give the credit for my longevity to the overruling of my God rather than to my rugged Scottish ancestors. Like many other Scottish and Irish families, my grandparents, both paternal and maternal, emigrated from Scotland to Canada in the nineteenth century, settling in southern Ontario. There my father met and married my mother, and there I was born on May 7, 1907, to be named Harold for reasons unknown and George after a favorite uncle. A sister, Florence May, had preceded me into the family seven years earlier.

The majority of the clan Mackay were staunch Presbyterians, including my grandparents; the Cramonds, my mother's family, were active Methodists. Their true spiritual condition is unknown to me, but through the gracious overruling of God, my parents were brought under the soul-saving influence of the gospel and had both been truly converted to Christ before they were married. They attended a small assembly of born-again believers who met in the Gospel Hall on Ainslie Street in Galt, Ontario, later to become the place of my spiritual rebirth. Thus I was reared in a home of Christian love and godliness, and from an early age was taken to hear the truth of God taught and preached in an evangelical assembly. These spiritual blessings far outweighed the humble circumstances of my birth and boyhood.

At the time of my birth, only the offspring of affluent parents entered the world amid the sanitized surroundings of a hospital maternity ward; others were born in the home of their parents, the mother being attended by the family physician. Inasmuch as my father was earning the princely sum of one dollar per day when he married, it is not surprising that my birthplace was a small tenement in what was known as the Terrace. I have no childish recollections of the place, so evidently the Mackay family moved elsewhere while I was still an infant. Did the lung power of the new arrival necessitate such a move?

My earliest memories are of a nice house in a middle-class neighborhood, where one of our neighbors was the city engineer. His wife and sons attended the same assembly as my parents. Evidently zoning laws were not as strict then as now, for a next door neighbor had a stable of horses behind his home. One Halloween night, a gang of us lads dismantled his wagon and carried it, piece by piece, to the top of his barn and reassembled it there, to the chagrin of its owner next morning and to the amusement of passersby.

In early adolescence, large for my age and well developed physically, I found myself associating with companions considerably older than I, and engaging in sports at the adult level. This had its snares, some of which I succumbed to. About this time Dad managed out of his meager earnings to purchase a large two-story house. It was a lovely home, with large rooms and a two-story veranda across the entire front. From the second story of this veranda, we had a wonderful view of the activities in the city park directly across the street, with its ballpark and recreation areas. It took but a minute or two to cross the street and engage in the baseball, softball,

16

soccer, football, lacrosse, and tennis games. Or, when interest in these paled, it was just one block to the country, with its open fields to roam in, streams to fish and swim in, berry bushes to strip, and maple trees to tap for maple sugar sap. There were camping spots and plenty of frogs to be caught for a feast of roasted frogs' legs!

All in all, it seemed to a growing boy an ideal location until one serious defect appeared. Behind the well-kept lawn, the apple, pear, and cherry trees laden with fruit, and the luscious berry bushes, was a large garden plot. My industrious Scottish father felt it was his parental responsibility to initiate his only son into the back-aching mysteries of gardening. That was long before the invention of the power-driven garden tiller, and it was hand (and hard) labor that made our garden one of the most productive in the neighborhood. Many a ball game in the park was interrupted by the sudden departure of one of the players (me!), called home to work in the garden.

Another flaw in the location of our new home ultimately appeared. Adjacent to the park was the acreage of a market gardener. The long neat weed-free rows of vegetables appeared very attractive to the casual passerby. But they little knew the weary hours of weeding by boys who earned a mere pittance for their labors. My prudent father decided this would be an excellent way for me to earn the spending money I was continually pleading for, and so I became an "assistant to the market gardener" instead of a future star athlete. My father had not heard of the astronomical salaries paid to athletes (nor had anyone else in those days), and so my future stardom was effectively stunted before it even began to blossom.

After we had settled in our comfortable home, another problem appeared to me. It was that spare bedroom, which quickly became the guest chamber for preachers visiting the local assembly. These were the old-fashioned type, who not only cast their nets from the platform, but seldom missed an opportunity to do a little hook-and-line fishing for individual souls. I was tempting bait for such. The guest room was also spacious enough to accommodate a number of extra beds at the Easter Conference, and each year it was filled to capacity with Christian visitors. This greatly increased my peril,

17

until in a burst of generosity I offered to give up my bedroom for guests, while I retired to the safety of my tent pitched on the bank of the nearby creek.

However, the pleasures of the playing fields in the park more than compensated for the pains of the vegetable fields; and roaming in the country and swimming in the spring-fed creek enabled me to forget boyhood problems. A new pleasure was added when a Boy Scout troop was organized in the neighborhood. Some natural ability, plus a lot of hard work, enabled me to secure promotion to the position of Troop Leader. This brought, along with other new experiences, camping trips to nearby points of interest.

Altogether, it was a happy boyhood. My parents were industrious and thrifty, and we were always well fed and clothed. Christian love and consideration pervaded the home atmosphere. There was strict discipline, which I resented at the time, but thank God for now. A carefree boy does not understand nor appreciate the concern for his spiritual well-being manifested by Christian parents and friends; but where might I have been today had it not been for that godly concern?

2
Education and Employment

Life is a learning process that commences in childhood and continues to old age. Some of the lessons are learned through the practical experiences of life and the application of basic principles, some in the structured environment of an educational institution. Both are necessary. Canadian law decreed I must attend school regularly; my parents were in full agreement, so off to school I went. This was before school busing and privately-owned autos were at a minimum, so we reached school by the "two-foot rule" (one foot in front of the other), anticipating the day we might own a bicycle.

The school system of my day in Canada was simple, sound, and strict. Attendance was compulsory five days a week from 9:00 AM to 4:00 PM with an hour break for lunch. Frigid weather and deep snows were not considered valid excuses for tardiness, let alone absenteeism. (Imagine my surprise, therefore, when many years later my own boys informed me there would be no school because it *might* snow! This was in the Southern states.) Discipline was strict, order prevailed in the classroom, and punishment for the infraction of rules was swift and sure. As a result, public school graduates left with a good basic education, well prepared for continued collegiate education or entrance into the business world.

Graduating from public school, I enrolled in the well-accredited Galt Collegiate Institute where I registered for the Teachers and Matriculation course, which provided the double option of entering the Normal School in Hamilton to prepare for a teaching career or of matriculating at the University of Toronto. Neither of these plans matured, as I dropped out of collegiate before graduating, much to the disappointment of my parents and of a maiden aunt, who envisioned me as an honor alumnus of the University of Toronto. None of my collegiate grade reports have survived, although I did unearth a brief report of my service as captain of the debating team, which may only indicate the presence of an argumentative disposition, which some of my peers claim has not entirely disappeared.

Beside the academic studies, there were gymnastics, basketball, and Canadian rugby, similar to American football. Then there was military training in the Cadet Corps at the school, with one week at army camp each year. I chose the medical corps with lectures under the shade of a tree, rather than marching on the drill field. We did manage to gain the trophy for our medical skill, plus a scathing lecture from the inspecting colonel for our sloppy uniforms.

While my parents were interested in a good academic education for their children, they were equally concerned that we become well instructed in Scripture truths. They recognized that "the fear of the Lord is the beginning of knowledge" (Prov. 1:7), and made every effort to instruct us in the way of salvation and the truths of the Bible. Our day in the home began with family Scripture reading and prayers, frequently supplemented by rather lengthy comments by preachers who were guests in our hospitable home. I still recall my pleasure at the practical exhortation by one preacher's wife: "Be brief, James. The children have to go to school."

Mother and Dad not only read the Bible to us, they "translated it into shoe leather" by their lives. This home education was supplemented by regular attendance at the assembly Sunday School. The Gospel Hall was limited in its facilities and did not have separate rooms for classes. However, temporary rooms were formed by placing benches in a square and suspending curtains on rods. These curtains were certainly not soundproof, and the occasional bulge in them betrayed a tantalizing point of attack on the anatomy of an unsuspecting neighbor. A muffled cry revealed the success of a pinch or pin. In spite of such diversions, we received sound instruction from the godly, dedicated teachers, who earnestly impressed on us the need of personal acceptance of Christ for salvation.

Completing workbooks that required Bible searching was rewarded with good Christian books, some still remaining in my library. That I was not saved earlier in life certainly was not the fault of my parents nor of my Sunday School teachers.

The offer of a position in the cost accounting department of a local firm, bringing with it the attraction of a much larger paycheck than I was receiving for my Saturday labors in a meat market, plus the increasing attention I was attracting as the protege of a popular professional boxer, lured me away from school, against the advice of wiser heads. In later years, I learned that this foolish mistake could only be rectified by long hours of private study over courses from LaSalle University.

It did not take very long for me to realize that work days were much more strenuous than school days; and even that larger paycheck did not secure for me all the satisfaction that I had imagined. If I had chafed under the discipline of firm school teachers, I now seethed under the arbitrary dictates of a domineering office manager. Rebelling against these unhappy working conditions and the restrictions of a Christian home, like many another teenager, I turned my eyes toward the "far country" of the big city of Toronto, sixty miles away. Surely there I would find freedom, fun, and fortune.

Taking advantage of a two-week vacation from the office, I went to Toronto, armed with a letter of recommendation from the secretary of the Galt YMCA. On the strength of that letter, I secured a position in the office of an international firm. A week's work there convinced me that it was a good move to make, so I returned to Galt and resigned from my job there. Naturally, my parents were apprehensive, but I had become increasingly restive and rebellious under the restraints of the Christian home. My father was a quiet, patient man, but no weakling. He had informed me that if I was too big to obey him in the home, I was big enough to paddle my own canoe. Seventeen years of age and possessed of an overblown ego, I felt quite capable of that. I proceeded to almost capsize my little craft!

In the metropolis of Toronto, one of Canada's largest and most progressive cities, I lived in a rented room with a family for a short time, then moved to a men's boarding house, where I was free to follow my chosen life of pleasure and folly. No good would be served by detailing the deeds of that deplorable part of my life when I mistook liberty for license and crossed quickly from the clean side of the broad road to the sordid ditch on the other side (Mt. 7:13).

I tried the broken cisterns, Lord, But ah! their waters failed!
E'en as I stooped to drink they fled, And mocked me as I wailed.

But even in those rebellious and riotous years, God's eye was on me and His hand preserved me. Stricken with ptomaine poisoning, I lay alone in my room, none of my so-called friends apparently caring whether I lived or died. However, God was merciful to me, having other plans for my life, and I recovered. If my worldly friends cared little, my Christian parents and friends cared much: their prayers followed me, and many unsuccessful efforts were made to interest me in spiritual matters. My godly aunt introduced me to her Christian friends, but I rejected all their overtures. My concerned mother traveled by train from Galt to Toronto to invite me to accompany her to the large Easter Bible Conference held in the spacious Massey Music Hall. I may have gone with her once out of courtesy, but I left the service unaffected. To one and all I took the obdurate stand, "I've charted my life's course, and there's no room in it for religion." Quite a mouthful for a seventeen-year-old! How much I had yet to learn. "Man proposes, but God disposes." I, like many others, was to learn the truth of William Cowper's words:

God moves in a mysterious way, His wonders to perform,
He plants His footsteps in the sea, and rides upon the storm.

True in the eighteenth century when Cowper wrote; just as true in the twentieth. God was about to graciously visit me with His salvation, completely alter my outlook, reverse my direction, and transform my behavior—all in one weekend! To do so, He would employ a newly-converted sister, many praying friends, a faithful soul-winner, and a holiday in honor of a British monarch. "Omnipotence hath servants everywhere." Many prayers were answered on May 23, 1926, and many bitter tears turned to tears of joy.

3
Conversion and Confession

"If thou shalt confess with thy mouth the Lord Jesus, and shalt believe in thine heart that God hath raised Him from the dead, thou shalt be saved" (Rom. 10:9).

Queen Victoria was one of Britain's most illustrious monarchs, reigning as Queen of Great Britain and Ireland and as Empress of India more than sixty years, longer than any other ruler in the history of her empire. During this long reign she was beloved of her subjects, and her memory has been revered since, being commemorated by a national holiday on her birthday in Canada and elsewhere in the British Commonwealth of Nations. What has this to do with my conversion to Christ? Just this.

Queen Victoria's birthday was on the 24th of May. In 1926 that date fell on a Monday, thus making a long holiday weekend. I decided to take advantage of these three days to pay a visit to my parents in Galt. This decision was not influenced in any way by recent correspondence from my home; rather, it was made in spite of the news contained in these letters. For several weeks I had been receiving letters from my parents and my sister bubbling over with the good news (to them!) of many conversions that were taking place in the Gospel Hall in Galt. These included my sister, her fiance Lorne Cochrane, and three of his sisters.

There could be no denying that a work of God was in progress in the little Gospel Hall on Ainslee Street in Galt—not the type of activity that secures headlines in the local newspaper nor wins popularity and prestige for the preachers, but a genuine movement of the

Spirit of God in convicting and converting sinners to Christ. The two men being used of God were assembly evangelists from Toronto. They presented a rather striking contrast in appearance, but made a very effective team. William Gillespie Sr., the older of the two, was a big burly man who had been an outstanding hammer thrower in his native Ireland before his conversion. He was not an educated man, but was a powerful preacher and a great soul-winner. His partner, Fred Nugent, was a handsome gentlemanly person in appearance and conduct. He was fluent and effective in his presentation of the gospel. Both were men of prayer and were deeply concerned for lost sinners. But they were merely the instruments God was using; the Spirit was working.

On my arrival home, I was invited to attend the services, but at first was adamant in my refusal to do so. But God has His own ways of working out His will. It was an arrow from a "bow drawn at a venture" that found the joint in the armor of King Ahab (1 Ki. 22:34), so it was a simple, but sincere, remark from Lorne Cochrane that first pierced my stubborn opposition to the gospel. As I passed the barbershop where he was employed, he came out, grasped my hand with a hearty shake and said with deep sincerity, "Harold, it's a grand thing to be saved!" I liked Lorne. He was a popular athlete, and he and Florence had enjoyed an active social life. Now he was talking warmly about the joy of being saved. Grand? Better than popularity and pleasure? I doubted it. But the arrow had penetrated!

After spending the Sunday afternoon regaling my former friends with a recital of my escapades in Toronto, I returned home to fulfill my reluctantly given promise to attend the gospel meeting at the hall, inwardly hoping that the family had all gone to the prayer meeting that preceded the gospel service. My parents had, but my recently saved sister had remained to prepare supper for me and thus deprive me of my last excuse. All the way to the meeting, an inward premonition gripped me that I was going to be saved, bringing to an end all my sinful pursuits and pleasures. I think I would have welcomed even an accident as a legitimate excuse for not attending. But we reached the hall, and I entered, fully determined to resist all efforts to convert me. Apparently my defiant attitude was so evident that it was remarked about later. But God was there, and I was no match for Him. It was not the preachers or the preaching that moved me that night. I had heard many preachers as sincere and earnest as those two, listened to many messages as clear and forceful as those preached that night; but never before had I been so deeply convicted of my sin, never had stood in such awe of Almighty God, never before trembled at the thought of eternal punishment. Under the convicting power of the Spirit of God, my stiff neck was bent, my proud heart was broken, and my head was bowed as tears of true repentance flowed down my cheeks. Seeing my conviction, yet knowing my trigger temper, my dear sister cautiously put her arm around me and whispered in my ear, "I'm sure you'll be saved if you stay behind." I had no thought of leaving; the matter had to be settled. It was that night or never.

When the preaching had ended, Brother Gillespie made his way to my side and, wise soul-winner that he was, began to probe and diagnose my condition and administer the balm of Gilead (Jer. 8:22). Together we read from his well-worn Bible the inspired revelation of the condition and cure, eventually reaching that Old Testament portion through which many a troubled soul has caught a soul-saving look at the Cross of Christ—Isaiah 53:5. Together we read: *"But He was wounded for our transgressions, He was bruised for our iniquities, the chastisement of our peace was upon Him, and with His stripes we are healed."*

"Can you put yourself into that verse?" I was asked.

"I can. 'But He was wounded for *my* transgressions; He was bruised for *my* iniquities, the chastisement of *my* peace was upon Him, and with His stripes *I* am healed.'"

"Are you healed by His stripes?"

"I will be if I believe." Ah! There was the stumblingblock!

It seems as though I can still see him reach into his pocket and bring out his pen which he handed to me with the request, "Will you please place that pen on the word *believe* in that verse." Of course I would. But it wasn't there. It must be! Had I not heard all my life

25

that salvation was by believing? I recall how, on a previous occasion, I had closed my eyes with the thought, "All right, I'll believe." With my eyes closed, I repeated several times, "I believe." Opening them, I found nothing had changed, so foolishly concluded there was no salvation in believing. Nor is there! It is not believing that saves, but Christ. And so, as I sat there with the pen in my hand, looking for the word *believe* in Isaiah 53:5, it was as though a great light had been turned on within me. It's not my believing that heals me; it's His stripes, and He received those stripes for me! I must shift my faith from my believing to His stripes.

"Will you receive this One who received the stripes for you as your personal Saviour and Lord?"

"I will. I do."

The good news quickly reached the praying group in the basement and up they came with radiant faces, led by my dear father who, with tear-stained cheeks, embraced his prodigal son now safely back from the far country of sin and rebellion. What a happy family went home that night, united in Christ in the heavenly family! Well do I remember our family prayer before we retired.

I wakened the morning after my conversion to discover that there were many lessons to be learned in God's school. At my conversion, I had learned the true nature of faith and that the *object* of faith was the all-important matter. Weak faith in the right object will bring salvation; strong faith in the wrong object will result in eternal loss. Now the first lesson I had to learn as a Christian was to distinguish between faith and feelings. This was basic, and would be needed throughout my entire life, not only for my own good, but for the help of others in my future service. I was keenly disappointed that morning to discover that the joy I had experienced at conversion seemed to have evaporated. Was I not saved? I sought my father who was already busy in his garden, taking advantage of the national holiday. His opening greeting was wisely chosen: "Well, son, are you still saved?"

"I'm afraid not, Dad."

"Why not?"

"Well, you see, I'm not as happy as I was last night."

Dad had been a student in God's school for many years, and he immediately recognized my problem. "Harold, what did that verse that you read last night say?"

"With His stripes we are healed."

"Are you healed from your sins by His stripes?"

"I certainly am."

"Didn't it say, 'With His stripes we are healed and happy'?"

"No, Dad, it didn't."

"Then never mind about the *happy*; just rejoice that you are *healed*. The happy will come later."—a valuable lesson I have re-called many times during the past sixty years and passed on to many others—"Be my feelings what they will; Jesus is my Saviour still."

On the train ride back to Toronto, I decided that I would say nothing about my spiritual rebirth, but would let my changed lifestyle witness to my conversion to Christ. I had yet to learn that true confession of Christ is a "show and tell" matter. To the deliv-ered demoniac, our Lord gave the double command: "Return to thine own house and *show* how great things God hath done unto thee" (Lk. 8:39); "Go home to thy friends and *tell* them how great things the Lord hath done for thee" (Mk. 5:19). It is by both lip and life we are to bear testimony to the transforming grace and power of God. But when the motive is right and the heart's desire is to honor the Lord, He prepares the way before us. So it proved in my case.

My roommate in the men's boarding house where I lived was big Jim, a young pleasure lover like myself, and he greeted me next morning with the usual, "Well, where are we going tonight, Mac?" It seemed I could hear my former boxing coach's favorite urging, "Take the offensive; don't let them get you on the defensive!" So I replied, "Sorry, Jim, I won't be going anywhere with you tonight. I became a Christian Sunday night." Jim exploded in an oath.

Going downstairs for breakfast, I stayed on the offensive and told the landlady about my encounter with Jim. She, like the Samar-itan woman at the well, immediately wrapped herself in a cloak of religion that none of us had ever suspected she had in her wardrobe.

27

"Oh, that's wonderful! I've always wanted to have someone ask the blessing at my table; now you can do it." I swallowed hard! This was a little more than I had expected. So at the dinner table she made the announcement, and I was faced with a group of unhappy, hungry men, impatient to attack their food. It was an acid test, and for some time I was faced with mostly empty dishes when I opened my eyes after a short prayer. But I kept at it, until finally the last holdout (a hard-bitten old sinner) capitulated and bowed his head with a show of respect.

Jim was waiting for me when I reached home after work with a sincere apology for his profanity in the morning. Many times after, when I would be leaving for work, he would say," Let them know who you belong to, Mac; you've got nothing to be ashamed of." Years later, I met Jim while travelling, and he wanted to show me a pornographic picture. As he held it in his hand, I reached into my pocket and drew out a gospel tract with which I covered it. He took one look at it and said, "Well, I see you're still at it!" I trust that my contact with Jim has resulted in his conversion; he would make an out and out witness for Christ.

Even more difficult than taking a stand before those I lived with was doing the same before those I worked with. This called for divinely-given wisdom and courage. Because my work was with the stock and shipping records, my desk was in the shipping room. Here my immediate associates were my supervisor, a nonpracticing Catholic, married to a Protestant wife; the shipping clerk, a pleasure-loving man of the world; the stock-truck driver, a foul-mouthed little English unbeliever; and the electrician, a big burly Jew who hated the name of Jesus. Rather a formidable foursome to present the claims of Christ to!

I had not been at my desk an hour when one of them called out, "What's the matter, Mac? You're not yourself this morning."

"No, I'm not myself; that is, not the old self you've known."

"Why, what's wrong?"

"Nothing. I was born again on Sunday." (Rather an unwise explanation!)

"You were what?"

"I was saved." (Still incomprehensible.)

"Why? Were you drowning?"

"No. I was converted." (A glimmer of light.)

"Oh, you've got religion."

Now was the opportunity to tell of my conversion in as simple words as possible (these were Canadian heathen.) After this verbal confession, the burden was on me to prove the reality of it. It wasn't difficult to determine what the change in lifestyle would be: no more partying with the clerk; no more nightlong beer and poker at the truck driver's home; no more poolroom at lunchtime; no more off-color jokes and profanity. But there must be more than a negative attitude; I must present the positive aspects of the true Christian life: love, joy, peace, patience, kindness, goodness, faithfulness, gentleness, self-control (Gal. 5:22-23). It was not a matter of "giving up," but of replacing the old with the new, which was better. I had an entirely new attitude toward life, new associates to company with, new activities to engage in, new aspirations to fulfill, an entirely different future to anticipate. "If any man be in Christ, he is a new creature; old things are passed away; behold all things are become new; and all things are of God . . . " (2 Cor. 5:17-18).

It was some time after leaving my employment with that company that I learned, by an unexpected incident, that my changed life had made some impression at least. Visiting in Toronto, I decided to drop in on the men I formerly worked with, and not wishing to go through the main office, I entered the shipping department by the side entrance. I was just in time to find the manager in the midst of a profane tirade against two unfortunate young employees. Seeing me, he stopped quickly and then rather lamely excused his profanity by saying, "Well, I was just telling these fellows what I thought of their complaint that they were expected to do too much work. I told them that I was just about to let a young man go because of his irresponsible attitude some years ago, when he claimed he had been converted and become a born-again Christian. From that time on, his work was so improved that he was doing what both of you are

29

doing today, and he had time, with my permission, to read his Bible in his spare time."

Beginning my new life as a Christian in Toronto, I realized my need of the fellowship of like-minded believers. I had not yet learned the truth of the one body of Christ and the interdependence of the members in that one body, but the Spirit within prompted me to seek the company of those who loved the Lord. What I had been taught in Sunday School, heard in the home, and now learned from my personal reading of the Bible, convinced me that the Christians who met at the hall in Galt were following the church pattern of the New Testament (and over sixty years of Bible study has confirmed this conviction), so I located one in Toronto, larger but otherwise similar to my home assembly. Visiting it, I was given a list of verses to read. These, I discovered, all related to baptism; so I returned to the elder and expressed a desire for baptism.

"Oh, you had better wait for a while," he said.

"Why? Don't you believe I'm saved?"

"Well, you seem to be."

"Am I doing anything a Christian shouldn't?"

"Not that we know of, but you had better wait."

He did not know that I had been reared in a Christian home where the imminent coming of Christ was a very practical belief. I said, "Do you believe that Christ may come at any time?"

"Certainly. He might come today."

"If Christ should come, will you accept the responsibility for me not being baptized for all eternity?"

"Bring your clothes on Wednesday night and we'll baptize you." And so I made the public confession of baptism.

I had still one difficult hurdle to cross in my early Christian life. Before my conversion I had been dating a young woman from a refined middle-class family. However, when I attempted to explain to her my spiritual experience, it was quite apparent that she was in total ignorance of Bible truth. I did my best to win her to Christ, speaking to her privately, taking her to gospel meetings, and praying constantly for her conversion, but although very respectful and congenial, she could not seem to comprehend what it was all about. Naturally, I was disappointed, and it was painful to sever our companionship, but God had other plans for me.

This was on the negative side; there must also be the positive. Toronto was sometimes termed "the city of churches," and among these were many fine evangelical groups. Many of these conducted regular Saturday night street meetings, as did the assembly where I was now fellowshipping. I asked to join them in this activity and will always remember the first such service I attended.

We formed a circle on the street corner and commenced the singing, testifying, and preaching. One of the brethren beside me whispered, "Wouldn't you like to give your testimony?" I responded with a brief account of my conversion. As we stood around at the conclusion of the meeting, a young woman approached me and said, "Excuse me, but I accepted Christ as my Saviour when you were speaking." What an encouragement! She was the first of many who have since gladdened my heart by a similar testimony. I have never seen her since, but hope to see her in heaven.

Among the Christians that I met at the Central Assembly was a young man about my age, who had moved to Toronto from western Canada with his widowed mother and two sisters. Having many mutual interests, including our sincere desire to live a life pleasing to the Lord, we became close friends. Adam was employed as a lithographer and owned a small car. Inasmuch as we were both free from our employment on Saturdays, we decided to use our free day visiting nearby towns and villages and witnessing for Christ. We purchased a good supply of gospel tracts and spent the Saturday afternoons distributing them from door to door, announcing an evening open-air service at a suitable location. There we sang and preached the gospel, giving our personal testimony.

And so the new life continued—new interests, new friends, new activities, new joy, and behind the happy life of active service was an equally happy private life of prayer and Bible study. My home study course in accounting from the university was replaced with a Scofield Bible correspondence course from the Moody Bible Insti-

31

tute in Chicago. There were edifying meetings at the assembly and happy fellowship gatherings in private homes. Always an omnivorous reader, I used every available minute to read helpful Christian literature. Now indwelt by the Divine Teacher (Jn. 16:13-14), I recalled with new appreciation much that I had heard in the past. Thus God was preparing me for my life's work, although I had no inkling of that at the time. The Lord also opened up the way for me to move from the worldly boarding house into the warm Christian home of a godly elderly couple who attended the same assembly as I. This was a tremendous advantage in my new life.

Possibly motivated more by youthful restlessness than by sound judgment, my friend from western Canada and I, along with another young brother in Christ, decided to quit our jobs and enroll in a harvest excursion that was taking workers to the prairie provinces of Canada to labor in the harvest fields there. Did I say *labor*? If we didn't know the meaning of that term before, we learned it the hard way there, from daybreak (or even before) to after sundown! It seemed like a foolish move, and that was the reaction of an elder to whom I mentioned our intentions. He replied by rather curtly quoting Proverbs 17:24, "The eyes of a fool are in the ends of the earth."

But to the West we went, joining a rather motley crowd of passengers on the excursion train, a crowd that was of such dubious nature as to warrant the presence of a watchful RCMP officer. We went through the coaches passing out gospel tracts, receiving in response a barrage of banana skins as we returned to our seats. Our first work experience in Manitoba was not too encouraging either. We hired out to a rancher with a 640-acre spread, but after twelve to fourteen hours in the field, the food was so skimpy that we packed our bags and moved on, hungry but wiser! The Lord was merciful to us and led us to a Christian farmer, whose wife not only fed us five (!) times daily (two in the field and three in the house), but who observed the Lord's Supper each Lord's day with a small group meeting in his farmhouse. What a break for stomach and soul!

At the end of the harvest I returned to my parents' home in Galt, deeply exercised as to the Lord's will for my life.

4
Call and Commendation

The deist's concept of God is that of an omnipotent Creator who brought the world into existence and then abandoned it to pursue its own course, without interest or intervention on His part. This notion is aptly described by Thomas Carlyle as "an absentee God, sitting idle since the first Sabbath." Happily, the Christian finds no such God portrayed in his Bible, but a caring God deeply concerned regarding the temporal, spiritual, and eternal well-being of His creatures. From its earliest pages, we find Scriptures filled with calls, invitations, and entreaties from the Creator to His creatures, from the heavenly Father to His family on earth. To the *sinner* comes the call to salvation, "Come unto Me" (Mt. 11:28); to the *saved* comes the call to separation, "Come out from among them" (2 Cor. 6:17); to the *son* comes the call to service, "Go work today in My vineyard" (Mt. 21:28); to some *servants* comes the call to some specific sphere of service, "Separate Me Barnabas and Saul for the work whereunto I have called them" (Acts 13:2). The secret of a successful and satisfying life lies in our response to the calls of God.

In the preceding chapter, I have briefly recorded my response to God's calls to salvation and to separation. The call to service seemed to come in a gradual manner. I have read with interest striking accounts of the call of some honored servants of Christ, but there was nothing of that nature in my experience. Rather, from the night of my conversion, I was firmly convinced that I now belonged to Christ, that my life was no longer mine but His to use as He saw best, and that it was now my responsibility and privilege to yield myself unreservedly to Him. I have referred in the preface to the deep impression made upon me by the little couplet "Only one life, 'twill soon be past, Only what's done for Christ will last." My response was a total commitment to live wholeheartedly for Christ. But how? That was my question now. Somewhere I came across a paraphrase of Proverbs 4:12 which read, "As thou goest step by step, the way shall open up before thee." This I took to be God's counsel and encouragement for me. If I would take by faith the step that He indicated, the next one would in due time be clearly made known to me. It was the message of the old-time footlamp, "light for one step at a time."

In the previous chapter, I have recounted some of the first steps I took in service for the Lord—witnessing in the boarding house, in the office, at the street-corner meeting, on the Manitoba excursion train, in the little assembly in the Manitoba farmhouse. These were small steps indeed, but they were taken in accordance with what I believed to be the will of God for me, in the way He was opening up before me, according to His promise. It has been wisely said and often repeated, "The longest journey begins with the first step." Even the Western trip, foolish as it seemed at the time, eventually proved to be a God overruled blessing.

My conversion brought an abrupt and complete withdrawal from dependence on nicotine and alcohol as stimulants, and this sudden termination of their artificial support had brought me to the verge of a nervous breakdown. The strenuous outdoor manual labor in the harvest fields was exactly what I needed, although I was unaware of it at the time. Also, when I returned to Galt, it was a blessing in disguise that office employment, necessitating mental strain, did not become available to me. I spent the winter in equally strenuous outdoor labor, cutting and hauling timber from the forest to the sawmill. The result was a strong body, steady nerves, and controlled emotions. I was now ready for another step, and once again the Lord opened the way.

The province of Ontario at that time was composed of three distinct areas from south to north. The southern area, along the shores of the Great Lakes, was the busy commercial and industrial region, with its financial and educational institutions and its largest cities. North of this was what was known as the Muskoka District. This was a delightful vacationland of wooded hills and peaceful valleys, interlaced with sparkling streams and lakes abounding with fish of many varieties, a favorite retreat from the rush and bustle of the southern area. Still further north was Northern Ontario with its forests, mountains, and mines. This was the rugged country of pioneer settlers, cultivating the virgin soil and serving as professional guides for hunters, trappers, and fishermen. It was rich in natural resources and challenged the pioneer spirit of a rugged breed of men and women.

Into this scene a young Scottish preacher had come some twenty years before the time of my conversion. He was a typical "chunk of granite" Scotsman, soon earning the respect of his peers by his feats of strength and endurance, particularly long lonely walks through the forest to reach isolated settlements and preach the gospel to the residents of such out of the way places. He had married and was living in Galt when I returned from my Manitoba trip. As I prayed about my future path, one morning I was strongly impressed to talk with him about the possibility of accompanying him on his next trip north. Walking the short distance from my father's home to his residence, I found him at home and was cordially invited in.

"What brings you here this morning, Harold?"

"Brother Lyon, I have been much exercised about my future, and am convinced the Lord has some service for me this summer. I was wondering if you planned a trip to the North this year, and if so, whether I could accompany you and distribute tracts and invitations, or serve in some other way. I have saved some of my earnings and could pay my way."

To my surprise, instead of answering me, he called to his wife in an adjoining room, "Martha, would you come here, please." When she entered, he said to her, "You remember when we were discussing our trip north this summer, it was suggested that we invite Harold Mackay to go along. Well, here he is now, inquiring as to our plans and whether he could accompany us. So this seems to be

35

the Lord's doing." And so arrangements were made for the trip and a departure date set. God had definitely shown me the next step.

Traveling north in Brother Lyon's car, we reached our destination safely and quickly obtained the use of a lakeside house, rent-free on condition that we paint it and reroof it. By the time we had covered those thirsty boards with paint, and shingled the roof, we fully realized that the term "free" was a misnomer! But Brother Lyon was no stranger to hard work. He had used a blacksmith's hammer before he was called to use the hammer of the Word (Jer. 23:29). How thankful I was now for the toughening of my muscles on the harvest fields and in the woods so that I was able to hold up my end of the work in a somewhat creditable manner. Nightly meetings were arranged in various places, the gospel was preached, and souls were saved. By the end of the summer of witnessing and working, my commitment to a life of service for the Lord had been fully tested by "on-the-job training." I knew now what laboring in the Lord's harvest fields meant.

Before we separated, I had two questions for Brother Lyon: first, what was his candid opinion as to my gift? Did he believe that I could be used of the Lord? Second, if so, what was his advice as to my next move?

His reply was, "Harold, I believe God can use you in the gospel if you are wholly committed to Him. Your spiritual father, William Gillespie Sr., is a wise and successful soul-winner. A period of service with him would greatly benefit you."

Encouraged by this, I approached Brother Gillespie at the first opportunity. He replied, "I am planning a trip to North Carolina in the southern United States. If your home assembly will commend you, I will be happy to have you accompany me."

The next step, then, was to meet with the elders of the Galt assembly. This I did, telling them of my exercise, my activities, and Brother Gillespie's offer. These elders had known me from childhood; most of them were in the service at which I was saved, and they had heard me preach on several occasions. After considerable questioning and a season of prayer together, they unanimously expressed their whole-hearted fellowship with me in launching out into the Lord's service, and they gave me a letter of commendation to this effect. This was, by no means, a license to preach, nor ordination papers, but an expression of introduction and of recommendation from godly elders who knew me, to those who were not acquainted with me. This was in keeping with the apostolic practice recorded in the New Testament (Acts 18:24-28; Rom. 16:1-2; 2 Cor. 3:12).

True to his promise, when Brother Gillespie received notification of my commendation by the Galt elders, he sent for me to join him in Oshawa, where he was commencing a series of gospel meetings. Here began another phase of my apprenticeship in the Lord's service. The preparatory years of many young preachers are usually spent in the classrooms of college and seminary. Profitable as such preparation could be, I am most thankful that God overruled for me to receive basic instruction under the tutelage of a godly soul-winner. With Brother Gillespie, I was to learn by example and exercise how to pray, to visit, to counsel with awakened sinners, and to bait the spiritual fisherman's hook to catch men and women, youths and children for the Saviour. Brother Gillespie was a man of prayer, and we spent many hours together in prayer for lost souls. I listened and learned as he answered the questions of the saved and unsaved that we contacted. He was a kindly, but candid, critic of my immature attempts at preaching the gospel. God graciously blessed our united efforts, and we rejoiced together over many souls won to Christ in the little assembly at Oshawa.

When we set out on the planned visit to North Carolina, God granted a further proof of His guidance and of His approval of my going forth in His service. Not realizing that a Canadian needed a visa for entrance into the States, I arrived at the immigration office near Port Huron, Michigan, without any papers. It was the year that Al Smith was running for President, and Catholic/Protestant feelings were tense. God overruled and I was checked by a staunch Protestant. Hearing the purpose of my proposed visit, and evidently impressed by my honesty and sincerity in the matter, he said, "If you go into the office, you may be turned back by one of Smith's Catholic friends; you stay here with me until your friend is cleared." This I did, and we were soon on our way to Asheville, North Carolina. Once again God had fulfilled His promise, "I will open up the way before thee."

In 1928, there was a very evident movement of the Spirit of God in the area around Asheville, in the mountainous western part of the state of North Carolina, and several preachers from the assemblies were led by the Lord to labor there. We took up our residence in a house with two of them, secured a wooden-sided tent heated by a large coal stove, and began preaching the gospel in a small town named Canton. God graciously honored the preaching of His Word, souls were saved, and we continued through the winter months.

Returning to Ontario in the spring, I joined William Gillespie Jr., who had been led to Christ by his father and had been commended to the work of the Lord. We labored together for two years, in assembly halls and in summer tent meetings, seeing many encouraging confessions of faith.

The winter of 1929 was spent in evangelizing a small village in the state of Maryland. Brother Gillespie and I rented and renovated an empty building and held nightly services for children and adults. There was a strong Roman Catholic element in the little village, evidenced on one occasion when I was giving an illustrated lesson to the children, using a glass of water. When I asked what was in the glass, one little girl replied, "Holy water."

When hot weather came, an adversary of the gospel rented the other half of the building and stabled several cows there. I need not explain why we quickly moved out! But the Lord worked and some strong cases of conversion took place.

It was here also that I learned the blessedness of obeying Paul's injunction in Philippians 2:4 where we are warned to give a high priority to the interests and needs of others. My fellowlaborer and several brethren from the nearby Lonaconing assembly were going to a Bible conference. How I longed to go with them and enjoy the fellowship and the ministry of the Word! But I had been visiting a young man dying from a terrible brain cancer, and I felt he was near conversion. I decided I must forego my personal desire to attend the conference and seek to win this dear man to Christ. When my brethren had left, I went to his home and once again put before him the claims of Christ. He asked me to sing, "Christ is the Saviour of sinners," which I did. When I came to the words, "Christ is the Saviour for me," an emaciated arm crept out from the bedclothes and a thin hand was pointed to his heart, as his twisted lips whispered, "Me!" I rejoiced with the angels in heaven over another repentant sinner saved by grace. What a rich recompense for relinquishing my visit to the Bible conference! I had learned that when we are willing to set aside our own desires for the good of others, the reward far exceeds what it may have cost us.

After the experience in this little village, I decided to purchase a gospel tent that could be erected in localities that seemed suitable for evangelistic efforts. While waiting for it to be made and shipped to us, we attended the Rhodes Grove Bible Conference in Pennsylvania. Here we sat under the edifying ministry of Brother Harold St. John, a gracious and gifted Bible teacher from England. There I also met A. P. Gibbs, with whom I was to enjoy a long association in the ministry of the Word at camps, conferences, Guelph Summer Bible School, and Emmaus Bible School.

When the new tent arrived, after much prayer for guidance, we pitched it in Aliquippa, a steel town in the Pittsburgh area of Pennsylvania. Here we preached the gospel for the remainder of the summer, God graciously blessing His Word to the conversion of a number of precious souls.

A rather amusing incident occurred one night when two men arrived at the tent and announced that they were members of the 144,000 (sealed as servants of God in Revelation 7). When I read the names of the tribes enumerated in Revelation 7, and enquired as to their tribal connection, they retired in silence.

5
Pioneering in West Virginia

It is a profitable study to trace in the Scriptures God's method of preparation of His servants. Of course, that preparation was particularly relevant to the service the Lord would call them to, but there were basic characteristics. Frequently the place of preparation was one of seclusion and solitude, away from the voices of men, that they might become sensitive to the voice of God. For Moses, it was "the backside of the desert" (Ex. 3:1-6); for Elijah, "by the brook Cherith" (1 Ki. 17:2-6); for John the Baptist, "the desert of Judea" (Lk. 1:80); for Paul, "Arabia" (Gal. 1:17); and for our Lord Himself, the obscurity of Nazareth (Lk. 2:39, 51; 3:23; 4:1-2, 14).

It is with extreme reluctance that I mention my own experience in the context of these great servants of God, but I am persuaded that the God of all grace is interested in the preparation of the least of His servants as well as the greatest. I had learned many profitable lessons from the brethren with whom I had been associated in my service for Christ, and was humbly grateful for the tokens of approval God had placed upon our united labors for Him; but that deep desire not to "build upon another man's foundation" (Rom. 15:20-21) continued with me, and I felt strongly urged to carry the truth into pioneer fields. God was now about to put that desire to the acid test by exposing me to some of the problems and privations of a pioneer field. Would I turn back as John Mark had done, or would I continue faithfully on, after the example of Timothy, as Paul testifies in Philippians 2:19-22 and 2 Timothy 4:9-10? The mountains and valleys of West Virginia were now to become my "backside of the desert," my "brook Cherith."

In 1931, I began to keep a daily diary, and I quote from a notation inserted in January of that year:

> Having inquired of brother W. G. Smith regarding opportunities to serve the Lord in the state of West Virginia, and receiving in reply a cordial invitation to join him in Huntington where he was residing, I left Toronto in company with William Gillespie, Sr., who would travel as far as Lonaconing, Maryland. Enroute we preached at Pittsburgh and Everett, Pennsylvania. Upon arriving in Huntington, I received a warm welcome from the Smiths and was invited to share in meetings in progress in a schoolhouse at Bear Creek, a small rural community a few miles from Huntington. Here we preached nightly; later at Branchland, Hamlin, and Peach Creek. Always interested in the conversion of children, I soon added special services for them three times each week, rewarding those who memorized a prescribed list of Bible verses with a highly-prized Bible. This period was a time of almost constant financial testing: I learned the value of pennies the hard way! And yet there were precious experiences of the providing care of God and of the joy of sharing our meager supplies with others. In one particularly pitiful case, a young unemployed father was unable to secure medical aid for his child stricken with scarlet fever, and the child died. We were asked to conduct the funeral. By draining the gas from one car to the other, we reached the post office where we found a letter waiting for us with S5 in it. The gas tank was replenished and the funeral conducted without anyone suspecting our financial condition.
>
> *(Synopsis of events from 10/16/30 to 1/1/31. Written 1/17/31 in Huntington, West Virginia)*

When I write of my Huntington experience as "the backside of the desert," it is not to suggest that I was lonely or without happy Christian fellowship. Far from it. The Smiths were most kind to me, and we shared our times of testing together, praying, reading, consulting, and laboring in a harmonious and profitable manner.

William Graham Smith was a true pioneer of the old school. Emigrating to America from his native Scotland as a young man, he settled in western North Carolina for health reasons. While pursuing his trade as a carpenter, he became deeply burdened about the spiritual need of those among whom he lived and worked, and began preaching the gospel. God blessed his efforts and souls were saved. He taught the new converts the New Testament church truths, and a small assembly was soon gathering in the Lord's name alone. Since a suitable building was not available, brother Smith took his carpentry tools and built a gospel hall. The Asheville assembly continues to this day in a new locality, with a new building and new faces, but on the biblical foundation laid by W. G. Smith. When he and Ruth Welstead were married, they decided to locate in West Virginia and there labor for the Lord in the mountain regions where both financial and spiritual poverty abounded. I had known the Welstead family in Toronto. William and Ruth Smith were both dedicated pioneers, deeply devoted to Christ and His work, and quite willing to forego many of the amenities of an easier life in order to carry the gospel to neglected areas of the country. If I had learned what a life of prayer was from William Gillespie, Sr., I learned what the price of a pioneer's life was from William Smith.

Before an assembly was planted in the area, the Smiths broke bread in their home with a few believers. Later, when an assembly testimony was begun in Huntington, brother Smith did most of the construction work on a small hall. Prior to this, he had remodeled his garage to make it suitable for children's meetings. Often the rural schoolhouses that we used for meetings had been unused for some time and repairs were needed on windows, doors, and benches. Brother Smith taught me some of his carpentry skill, and together we labored in work as well as in the Word.

I also learned other skills, such as how to drive my car up the bed of a mountain stream when no road existed; and when that trail ended, we often reached our destination by the "two-foot rule" (one foot in front of the other). The "body-building course" I had taken

43

on the harvest fields of Manitoba stood me in good stead now in our rigorous life, and the healthy appetite I had developed there delighted the country cooks who took great pride in seeing their "vittles" rapidly consumed by the young preacher. I secured many a promise to come to the night service in the schoolhouse by working with the men in the field. They actually derived more amusement than advantage from the preacher trying to guide a mule-drawn plow between the rows of corn. But I didn't mind being laughed at when it won an opportunity to preach the gospel to them. And when stir-off time came for making sorghum molasses, my expertise with an axe and a saw, learned in the Canadian woods, gained their respect.

All in all it was an interesting chapter in my life. Only eternity will reveal the fruit from those labors, but even now God gives an occasional "handful on purpose" to encourage. Just last year, more than fifty years after the time I am writing about in West Virginia, my phone rang: "Is this brother Mackay?"

"Yes, it is."

"Are you a preacher?"

Convinced that he had the right party, the caller continued, "Brother Mackay, I live in the state of Oregon. I was saved more than fifty years ago, lying on the grass outside your tent in Hamlin, West Virginia. Now my wife and family are saved, and some of the grandchildren."

So once again the promise had been fulfilled: "Cast thy bread upon the waters, for thou shalt find it after many days" (Eccl. 11:1) and "Let us not be weary in well doing, for in due season we shall reap" (Gal. 6:9).

Not only my physical stamina was put to the test in those days, but also my spiritual strength. This latter test usually came in the form of straitened financial circumstances. If the reading of such diary entries as the following creates some amusement now, the writing of them produced none then: "Balanced receipts for Jan.—$20.00. Combined cash on hand—27 cents. Gas about done in tank—S5.00 gift in mail. Mailed Exam #3—postage 4 cents—3 pennies left."

44

Obviously such an income left little for food. One rather amusing incident comes to mind. We had our gospel tent pitched in a rural community and were "baching" nearby. There was always a good supply of fresh vegetables and eggs, and when some delicious-looking country ham was given to us, we decided some toast would be good with it. The trouble was that we did not have enough cash on hand to purchase a loaf of bread. Remembering that I had seen some small loaves, I hurried off to the country store to try to find one within our means. Sure enough, there was one at the back of the shelf, and I was soon happily on my way home with it. But reaching our bachelor quarters and unwrapping it, we found it—moldy! Oh, well, somewhere I had read that penicillin was a mold; so, hoping this was the right kind of mold, we decided to toast it rather heavily and eat it. It is surprising what a thick layer of homemade apple butter or sorghum molasses will do to change the taste of moldy bread and burnt toast! At least the "West Virginia penicillin" didn't shorten our lives, for Brother Smith was in his 90's when he went home to glory, and I am in my 80's and still living as I write this in 1990.

But if our earthly funds were meager, we were able to rejoice in our spiritual riches in Christ, and we felt an empathy with Paul when he wrote, "As poor, yet making many rich; as having nothing, yet possessing all things" (2 Cor. 6:10).

Although, as I have stated, we were kept busy with many activities, I realized the danger of neglecting my personal spiritual needs. I tried to keep in mind the warning: "Beware of the barrenness of a busy life." Fortunately, Brother Smith was a man of prayer, so we had many precious sessions at the throne of grace together. My diary also records much time spent in Bible reading and study, including the completion of the profitable Scofield Bible Course from the Moody Bible Institute, as well as many Christian classics such as MacIntosh's *Notes on the Pentateuch,* Gaebelein's *Annotated Bible,* McConkey's *Threefold Secret of the Holy Spirit,* and many more of equal interest and profit.

This period of pioneering continued through 1932, and I owe much to the kindness, consideration, and counsel of William and

Ruth Smith. They did much to increase the spiritual usefulness of the young preacher. It has been a great joy during recent years to have them near us in North Carolina laboring for the the Lord until Brother Smith's homecall.

6
A Lifetime Partner

"And the Lord said, It is not good that a man should be alone; I will make him an help meet for him . . . and the Lord God made a woman and brought her unto the man" (Gen. 2:18, 22).

I had received many rich spiritual benefits from laboring in company with gifted and godly servants of Christ, but now the Lord was going to give me a lifetime partner and companion, one with whom I would share not only my labors for the Lord, but a love that would last a lifetime and be surpassed only by our united love for Him.

Few readers of Chapter 5 will expect to find a wedding in Chapter 6! It will come as a surprise to most to discover that the young pioneer preacher who was experiencing such testing times among the mountain people of the Appalachians was now considering asking a young woman to share those straitened circumstances with him. And it may come as a greater surprise to find a beautiful young woman, gainfully employed, living in a comfortable home with her Christian parents and family, who would accept such a proposal. But that is exactly what transpired; for that is love, especially true Christian love.

Gertrude Marjory Eckert had been saved a few years prior to my conversion. She had been reared in a Christian home, but did not accept Christ as her personal Saviour until she attended meetings in her home city of Kitchener, conducted by a Christian businessman from Toronto. From the time of her conversion, although only fifteen years of age, she manifested a real concern for the salvation of others, visiting hospitals and distributing tracts. When she approached an elder of her home assembly asking to be permitted to teach a class of girls in Sunday School, he told her that no class was currently without a teacher. Undaunted, she decided to gather her own. To do so, she went into poorer sections of Kitchener where there were many unchurched children, visited their homes and gained permission from several girls' parents to take them to Sunday School. On Sunday mornings she would go from door to door, gathering up her charges, who were often wearing clothes she had bought for them, and take them by streetcar to the Gospel Hall. She had the joy of leading many of these girls to the Lord, an early taste of future blessing in soul-winning.

Her mother was a kind, caring woman, always ministering to those in need, so Gertie was often sent with a basket of fresh-baked bread or pies for some sick person. Her father, who had left a well-to-do family in Germany at the age of seventeen to emigrate to Canada, was a real trophy of the saving and transforming power of the grace of God, a fearless faithful witness for Christ, frequently preaching the gospel on the street corner, his young daughter standing beside him. In all this, and in many other ways, God was preparing Gertie for her life's work as my faithful co-laborer for Him. Taught by the instruction and example of her godly parents, early in life she learned to honor the Lord with her money, setting aside the Lord's portion regularly, and sending some overseas to missionaries on the field. One well-known missionary, home on furlough in Canada, diligently sought out "the young girl" whose gift had reached him at a most opportune time. That young girl was my future wife, although at that time she had no way of knowing that she and her husband would be supported for over sixty years by just such unsolicited gifts from exercised Christians.

Returning to my home city of Galt after my trip to western Canada, recounted in Chapter 3, I attended a Bible conference in the nearby city of Hamilton where I met Gertie. We saw each other frequently during the conference and enjoyed one another's company. Later I was invited to visit her family in their home, which I did. The visit enabled Gertie and me to spend considerable time together, and we became increasingly drawn to each other. Interest deepened into affection and affection into true love, and we became convinced that we were intended by God to become life partners.

During the late summer months of 1931, I had my gospel tent pitched in the rural communities of West Hamlin and Salt Rock in West Virginia, preaching nightly and two or three times on Sundays. I lived in a small tent pitched nearby, subsisting in the main on meals cooked by myself. Needless to say, the menu was not elaborate or varied. When funds ran low, which was normal, the food was whatever friends sent in. Those were the circumstances under which, on August 30, I wrote to Gertie proposing marriage the next month! We had been corresponding regularly, so she was well aware what the conditions of our life were apt to be. Her reply came back accepting the proposal, to my great relief and joy. Although her parents had suggested that we wait another year, I left for Canada on September 25, hopeful of returning with my bride. After visits in Maryland and Pennsylvania with Christian friends, I arrived in Galt on October 18.

After a brief visit with my parents, I hurried to Kitchener to present in person the marriage proposal I had made by mail to Gertie. I read to her the words of Ecclesiastes 4:9-12:

"Two are better than one, because they have a good reward for their labor; for if they fall, the one will lift up his fellow. But woe to him that is alone when he falleth; for he hath not another to help him up. . . . And if one prevail against him, two shall withstand him; and a threefold cord is not quickly broken."

I strongly urged her that we become the two referred to in that passage, believing God could use us together for His glory. She accepted, and we decided on a date in November.

On November 25, 1931, in a private ceremony attended by our families and a few close friends, we were united in marriage in the home of Gertie's parents in Kitchener. Brother Thomas Touzeau, a preacher from Tillsonburg, Ontario, officiated. Then about twenty sat down to a delicious wedding dinner (quite different from my West Virginia fare!) In keeping with her personal wish, Gertie had made her own wedding cake, although her mother had it professionally decorated.

The following day being the American Thanksgiving, the American consulate was closed, so we were obliged to wait until the 27th to secure Gertie's visa; then crossing the border at Niagara Falls, we drove to Pittsburgh. I proudly introduced my bride to my many Christian friends there. We were showered with every kindness, including a bridal shower in which we received many of the practical necessities for setting up a home. Then we drove on to Lonaconing, Maryland, where I was scheduled to hold two weeks of meetings. This was Gertie's introduction to many such services together in years to come, with me doing the platform preaching, her listening and praying. I am sure that the prayer had as important a share in such services as the preacher.

Then it was on to Huntington, where we were warmly welcomed by Mr. and Mrs. Smith and the local believers. For some time, brother Smith had wanted to visit his aged mother in Scotland. With us back in Huntington to carry on the work, it seemed a good opportunity for him to fulfill this desire, and so it was arranged that Mrs. Smith and the children go to Toronto to visit her folks there, while he went to Scotland. We were invited to occupy their house on Overlook Drive, which we agreed to do, insisting over their objections that we make the mortgage payments during their absence in lieu of rent. Thus God's hand was again evident in making necessary provision for us. Soon we were busy with a full schedule of meetings for young and old in Huntington, Bear Creek, Hamlin, Hickory Ridge, Gallipolis, and elsewhere. Gertie's previous experience in visitation enabled her to fit in immediately. The women, particularly, took to her warm and outgoing personality.

There were testings of course, financially and physically. Gertie contracted measles while visiting a Sunday School girl, so I had a brief course in practical nursing. Then I had a severe bout with neuritis, and I became the patient and she the nurse. I have previously referred to the extreme poverty of the people in the rural areas. Gertie had purchased a lovely fur coat when employed in Kitchener.

Feeling it to be out of place in the homes we were visiting, she sent it back to her mother in Canada, the first of many such amenities she cheerfully relinquished for the Lord's sake.

Another type of test soon arose for Gertie. After only six months of marriage, in May of 1932 we were joined in our labors for the Lord by Edwin Fesche, who had been commended to the work by his home assembly in Baltimore, Maryland. A former sailor in the Merchant Marine, he was a rugged individual who fit well into pioneer work. I wondered, however, how my young bride would respond to finding herself responsible for the feeding of two hungry preachers. But she rose nobly to the occasion. She had been reared in a Christian home by hospitable parents who often entertained preachers and missionaries in the home for short or longer periods of time. Calling on this early training, Gertie saw to it that guest and husband never went hungry. She accomplished this on a slim budget, carefully scanning the one newspaper a week for food bargains! During the eight months that he remained with us, Brother Fesche and I held meetings in country churches, tents, schoolhouses, and in a building we rented in the Guyandotte area of Huntington.

Gertie's role in our work went far beyond her talents as cook, homemaker, and hostess, however. Saved in her early teens, she had acquired a good knowledge of the Scriptures, which she soon began to use in many ways with children, youths, and women. In each place where we have lived, she has taught Bible classes for such; many Christian mothers and grandmothers today were led to Christ by her in those classes.

A little more than two years after our marriage, Gertie took on another role. God gave us our firstborn on March 30, 1934, a nine pound son with his mother's auburn hair and brown eyes, whom we named John after my father, and Harold for me. Three years later, in the same city of Bristol, Virginia, his brother arrived, to be named Stanley after a little brother of mine who had died at birth and Richard after Gertie's father. Several years later, in 1945, when we were living in Greensboro, North Carolina, our family was completed by a third son, Ronald George. These boys, Jack, Stan, and Ron, brought much joy to our hearts and home, and increased our dependence on God for their provision, protection, and instruction. The full responsibility often fell on Gertie during my many absences from home on service for the Lord, and their conversion in early life can be attributed largely to her loving, prayerful rearing of them. They early learned never to leave the home without her prayer with them. In later years, Stan often chuckled at the memory of keeping one eye nervously fixed on the approaching school bus as his mother's unhurried prayer for protection and blessing continued.

During the busy years of child-rearing, entertaining guests, joining me in visitation, and maintaining many other responsibilities in the local assemblies where we served, Gertie often found it difficult to reserve a daily personal time with her Lord. Knowing that this was a necessary source of spiritual strength for the day, she became very resourceful in finding ways to do this. On summer mornings during our years in Greensboro, a secluded spot in a wild-flower garden she had planted was a favorite early morning retreat. At times, however, escaping from the constant telephone calls and the rough-and-tumble of three growing boys demanded more creativity. Our sons still tell of the time their unanswered calls for her to arbitrate some childish dispute finally led them to the toolshed where she perched calmly on an up-ended crate with her Bible.

Parents never fully realize the impression their daily lives make on their children. When our oldest son was being interviewed for a position with a large firm, the company psychologist asked him about his parents' occupation and salary. He answered, "My father receives no salary."

"Doesn't that give you a feeling of insecurity?" asked the startled interviewer.

Jack's reply: "I feel more secure knowing that my mother and father are praying for me than if we had a large income."

7
Teaching and Preaching in Virginia

"At the commandment of the Lord they rested in the tents; and at the commandment of the Lord they journeyed" (Num. 9:23).

After more than two years of laboring for the Lord in the Huntington area, Gertie and I began to feel the growing conviction that the Lord had a move elsewhere for us. But we did not want to mistake the restlessness of the flesh for the movement of the pillar cloud, so we gave ourselves to much prayer on the matter.

To the south of us, in Virginia, God had been blessing the preaching of two brethren, David Blackburn and Frank Detweiler. Souls had been saved and two small assemblies planted in Bristol and Marion. Brother Blackburn was killed in an auto accident, and on January 7, 1933, Brother Detweiler wrote inviting me to join him in Bristol. Was this the Macedonian call (Acts 16:9-10)? We prayed daily about this important decision. By February of 1933, we had decided that I should go to Bristol while Gertie remained in the Smith home, to which we had moved during their absence in Canada. Putting out two "fleeces" (Jud. 6:36-40), we asked the Lord to indicate clearly if it was His will for us to locate in Bristol; first, by granting blessing in my meetings there with souls being saved, and, second, by directing me to suitable and affordable housing for us.

Arriving in Bristol on March 4, with some difficulty I located the chapel, a small wooden building in a rather poor section of the city with the somewhat pretentious name of Kingtown. Nearby in Peace Cottage lived two godly women, Miss Marian Henwood, an English lady, and Miss Marietta Middleton, a former missionary to India.

These two carried on a most commendable work with the women and children in the district. I spent several hours in happy fellowship before hurrying to the chapel for the prayer meeting. After the meeting, the brethren remained for conversation and better acquaintance. Then I retired to the one-room "worker's apartment." This was adequate, but not exactly Holiday Inn standards! A single bed provided sleeping accommodation, a coal stove served the double purpose of heating and cooking, and a table and one chair constituted the dining area. Tired from my travel, I settled down on the lumpy mattress. For the next month, I cooked, ate, and slept there while conducting a full schedule. At schools I spoke to the children, preached in a denim factory, visited many homes during the day, each night conducted a service for children, then for adults at the chapel, attended services at the Marion Chapel on weekends before hurrying back to Bristol for the Sunday night service.

At the conclusion of the first night's service in Bristol, a woman professed faith in Christ, and thus the first fleece was quickly fulfilled. This initial conversion was followed by several more, most encouraging to me and to the local believers. Meanwhile I was looking for suitable living quarters, and the Lord eventually led me to a four-room apartment in the home of a dentist's widow, which I was able to rent for $15.00 per month. Thus God gave us the second fleece. Although the meetings in the Kingtown Hall were not large to begin with, interest and attendance increased until on the closing night extra seating was required. This, along with a good number of professions of faith, seemed convincing evidence that God was leading us to Bristol. This conviction was further confirmed by two letters received at this time: one from brother Smith informing us that they were returning to Huntington on April 7, the other from Frank Detweiler inviting me to join him in tent work during the summer in Johnson City, Tennessee, just a few miles from Bristol.

While there was not the poverty in the Kingtown district that we had encountered in the Appalachian Mountains of West Virginia, it was certainly not an affluent neighborhood. Most of the personal gifts we received ranged from 50 cents to $2.00; fellowship passed on from the assembly was about $10.00. This would certainly prove that we were not lured by financial gain in making our move to Bristol; we were convinced it was the leading of the Lord. So on April 6 I packed the car for the return trip to Huntington. The following day, the Smiths arrived from Canada. After our wives had retired for the night, W. G. and I conversed until 3:00 AM, he relating his experiences on the trip and the blessing of the Lord on the meetings held in the Pape Avenue Gospel Hall in Toronto, where over forty had professed; I bringing him up to date on the work in the Huntington area and relating the Lord's guidance in connection with our proposed move to Bristol. What a happy time of fellowship as we rejoiced together in the Lord's goodness to each of us!

On April 9, Gertie and I drove to Bristol, where we received a warm welcome from the Misses Henwood and Middleton. On Monday, we moved into our apartment at 525 Goodson Street. Our landlady Mrs. McElrath was a cultured, friendly Virginia lady, and she welcomed Gertie almost as a daughter, a congenial relationship that continued during our entire stay in Bristol.

Settled into our new living quarters, I launched into a full schedule of meetings for children and adults, in some schools, a local factory, and at the chapel. Special gospel meetings in the Kingtown Hall resulted in some very encouraging conversions. Then a series of meetings at the Marion assembly produced further fruit in the gospel, as did also similar services at Seven Mile Ford near Marion. God was putting His stamp of approval on our move to Virginia and we rejoiced. The Christians were instructed in the basic Bible truths and in New Testament church principles and practices. Baptisms were held in several places. I was convinced that the Great Commission (Mt. 28:19-20) included evangelism, immersion, and instruction; I have adhered to this throughout my life of service.

A visit from James Spink was very enjoyable to the Christians, and it refreshed us personally. He was a good man, gifted in the Scriptures, one of many such godly fellow servants of Christ it has been my privilege to know and labor with: "There were giants in the land in those days." In these days, when many are attacking New

55

Testament church principles and practices and seeking to tear down what stalwarts for the truth have stood for in years gone by, I often think of the words of Psalm 74:5-6: "A man was famous according as he had lifted up axes upon the thick trees. But now they break down the carved work thereof at once with axes and hammers." Demolition is much easier than construction.

Just a short drive from Bristol, across the line in the state of Tennessee, was a place brother Frank Detweiler had been exercised about, and early in June of 1933, we pitched his tent in Johnson City, setting up his small camper under a tree for our living quarters. We canvassed a considerable area with handbills announcing the meetings and commenced morning services for children and evening gospel meetings for adults. Attendance was not large at first, but increased as we continued; there were professions of faith in Christ and some very promising contacts were made. Among these were two brothers from a well-known business family. The oldest son and his sister were engrossed in a successful retail business career, but their two brothers became diligent in the Lord's business and were a real joy and encouragement to us. They attended the services regularly. The older of the two later moved to Florida, where he became active in one of the assemblies there.

We had a brief but most enjoyable visit from Harold St. John, a gifted Bible teacher from England. While he was with us in Johnson City, we were able to arrange a Bible reading for him in the large home of a local socialite who was a dear Christian lady.

At the second location where we pitched the tent, interest was much better, attendance reaching the 200 mark on some occasions. As we taught the truths of believers' baptism, and gathering in church fellowship in the name of the Lord Jesus Christ, there was so much interest that we soon arranged for a baptismal service by damming up a creek on a brother's farm. An unexpected torrential rain tore away this dam, but we built a more substantial one, and a fine crowd gathered on a Sunday afternoon to witness a number of believers publicly profess their identification with Christ in His death, burial, and resurrection.

56

Learning of the weekly observance of the Lord's Supper at the Kingtown assembly in Bristol, some of the Johnson City families began to attend it. By the fall of 1933, there seemed to be suitable "living stones" on hand for the commencement of a New Testament assembly. A Christian barber who had been attending offered to rent us his barber shop for $8.00 per month. We signed a lease for two years, remodeled it, and opened it as Grace Gospel Hall.

There were now four small assemblies to nurture in the ways of the Lord: Johnson City, Bristol, Marion, and Seven Mile Ford. Our objective was to see them expand numerically through souls being saved by gospel preaching, grow spiritually in a deeper knowledge of the Word and ways of God, then mature into indigenous local churches with God-given gifts. To this end, special gospel services were held in each place, and we were encouraged when there were professions of faith in Christ that proved to be genuine conversions. These were baptized; then ministry was given regularly of such a nature as to promote growth. There was keen interest in several series of studies I gave, such as *The Tabernacle in the Wilderness,* and requests for notes led to mimeographed outlines which were widely circulated. A monthly *Bible Study Letter* further stimulated personal study of the Scriptures. In each assembly we sought to develop a Sunday School program. To assist the teachers, I prepared and mimeographed Sunday School lessons. When any of the brethren gave evidence of a Spirit-given gift in the preaching and teaching of the Word, I spent many hours with them, instructing them in the preparation and delivery of edifying messages.

We began a Sunday afternoon broadcast from the Bristol radio station, held street meetings on Saturday nights in Marion, held school and shop meetings on many weekdays, and maintained a busy schedule of visitation in homes and hospitals.

Among the out-of-town visitors to our tent meetings in Johnson City had been Dr. Innes, a Christian physician who had set up a practice in the mountain town of Pennington Gap. Having been associated with assemblies elsewhere, and being a well-taught Bible student himself, when he heard of our meetings he visited us on several occasions, urging us to bring the tent to his town.

Pennington Gap is located in Lee County, one of Virginia's western counties, adjacent to Harlan County in Kentucky. The infamous twenty-year feud between the Kentucky McCoys and the West Virginia Hatfields had earned for the Kentucky county the unenviable designation of "Bloody Harlan." While not as notorious as Harlan, Lee County was a rugged mountainous area, inhabited by poor but fiercely independent people. The prevalence of "mountain dew" and shotguns, coupled with an ingrained suspicion of strangers, created a rather uncertain atmosphere for "outsiders." On the other hand, the people were generous and hospitable, and once their confidence was gained, they were the most loyal of friends.

No Saturday meetings being scheduled in Johnson City, brother Frank Detweiler decided to accept Dr. Innes' invitation and visit the Gap. He arrived at a most opportune time. A large crowd had gathered at the train station to view a travelling exhibit which had been brought in on a flatcar. Not one to miss an opportunity, he immediately commenced to preach the gospel to the curious crowd. The general reaction appears to have been favorable: we later met and led to Christ a hard-drinking miner who had surprised his wife when he reached home that day by informing her that he had heard preaching that suited him, and he would certainly go and hear that preacher again if he ever came to town!

"Assuredly gathering that the Lord had called us for to preach the gospel unto them" (Acts 16:10), we took down the tent at Johnson City and trucked it to Pennington Gap early in August of 1934. We pitched it in a central location and covered the town with announcements of the services. My first introduction to the locals was not so successful as Frank's had been. Curious to see how far the preaching could be heard outside the tent, I strolled around the adjoining streets while he was preaching, only to learn the following morning that my actions had aroused the suspicions and anger of one of the local doctors. As a result, he had made a threat against my life. I had learned from my West Virginia experience that the best way to deal with such situations involving mountaineers is by a friendly face to face confrontation, so I visited the doctor in his office. He arrogantly rejected my polite explanation and threatened to shoot me if I approached his residence again. I quietly reminded him that the sidewalk beside his house was public property, and that if I had legitimate reason for walking that way, I intended to use the sidewalk, not the road. His reply was a threat to throw me out of his office. The Lord graciously controlled my pre-conversion pugilistic reaction, and I left, crossed the street to where the chief of police was standing, and explained the matter to him. He was most cordial and apologized for the doctor's behavior. I later learned that the whispered rumor in those parts was that the doctor had shot his own father, so the Lord obviously mercifully preserved me.

After such an ominous introduction to the town, however, we had splendid meetings in the tent, in spite of the fact that the local ministers held a united meeting and decided to boycott the tent campaign. The devil seldom bothers those who are not bothering him, so we took courage and continued for two months, six nights a week. Souls were saved, including the miner who had first heard Frank preach at the railway station. Much later he told me he had no difficulty in believing the miracle of the Lord turning water into wine. "Look around this house," he said; "the Lord turned liquor into all this furniture, for we had very little when I was unsaved." Thus God's gospel transforms lives.

On another occasion, as the opening hymns were being sung, a miner called to me, "Preacher, sing that song about being on time." So we sang the solemn words:

> Life at best is very brief, like the falling of a leaf,
> Like the binding of a sheaf; Be in time.
> If in sin you longer wait, you may find no open gate,
> And your cry be just too late; Be in time.

A very short time after, it may even have been the next day, the news that chills hearts in a mining community spread through the town: "There's been a rock fall in the mine!" With many others, I hurried to the pit's mouth, only to find that one of the victims was the miner who requested the hymn. I hope he was in time.

Some of the conversions in the tent meetings were truly remark-able. I well remember being told by a bystander who was watching us put up the tent, "Well, there's one man in town who'll never enter this tent. J. R. has never entered a church in his life and he never will." But enter the tent J. R. did, and God spoke to his hardened heart. He accepted Christ as his Saviour while working deep in the mine pit. He was totally illiterate, could not read his own name, but God put into his heart a desire to see others saved. He gathered a group of children under a tree in his yard for a Sunday School class. He would ask one of the children to read from the Bible, then he would talk to them from the verses read. He did not know the alphabet, but he knew the way of salvation; many a Ph.D. does not.

Then there was the young lad who was saved in the tent meetings and who soon after informed me that he was having meetings in his home community. Would I come and preach one night? Certainly. So we drove up a "hollow" as far as we could in my car, parked it, and I followed him up a steep incline to a little clearing in the woods where a small company of people were seated on home-made benches. Around the circle he had planted short poles, each one holding a miner's lantern. This was the lighting system for the service, aided by the lanterns worn on the heads of many of the men present. When I rose to speak and looked around at that primitive scene, I asked myself, "This is *America?*" Then I thought, "Change the faces, dress, and surroundings, and you have such a gathering as our Lord addressed many times during His earthly ministry. And such a service as many missionaries conduct in foreign lands." What a privilege to proclaim Christ to these sincere people!

Not only did we have the privilege of heralding Christ's salvation in Lee County, but I was able to cross into Kentucky and preach in the former hometown of the notorious "Devil Anse" McCoy, the widely-feared leader of the feuding Kentucky clan.

In Pennington Gap, we enjoyed precious fellowship with Dr. and Mrs. Innes. They were both well versed in the Scriptures and had many years of Christian experience, so that we learned much from them. By this time we had become acquainted with a small but enthusiastic group of believers who began to meet regularly in the Innes' home for the Lord's Supper and Bible study.

These were busy and happy days, filled with service for others on behalf of our Lord who had said when on earth, "I am among you as He that serveth" (Lk. 22:27). Gertie found her life just as full as mine, with homemaking, caring for the two sons God had given us by this time, often visiting with me, and instructing children, youth, and women. Added to the daily family devotions were many hours of Bible reading on my part and the study of home Bible courses, English grammar, and New Testament Greek. Glancing over the pages of my diaries for that period, I note the number of classic Christian volumes I took time to read, often far into the night. Those were formative years.

For four years we continued in Bristol, but toward the end of 1937 there seemed to be increasing indications that the Lord might be preparing us to move. We prayed about this, taking the Lord's people into our confidence for their prayers and counsel. Gertie and I decided to put out our two "fleeces" again. I would accept the invitation to hold meetings in Marion; we would look to the Lord to bless those meetings with conversions and also lead to a suitable residence for us, if it was His will for us to locate there.

A Bible conference had been scheduled in Marion for July 4-5, with John Bramhall and Dr. Moomaw as the speakers. It proved to be a time of spiritual blessing. We had brought the tent from Pennington Gap to Marion for the conference, so afterwards I commenced nightly gospel meetings. Each Saturday night we held an open-air meeting on the main street, attended by as many as 200 people. Attendance at the tent meetings increased, and after about two weeks of preaching and much prayer, the Lord began to work and souls were saved in the tent and in homes.

One day I picked up a hitchhiker just outside the city. He did not recognize me, so I asked him if he had been to the tent meetings. He answered emphatically, "Just once, but no more!"

"Why?" I inquired.

61

"When I attend my own church, I get a good sleep during the sermon, but after hearing him, I couldn't get to sleep for hours!"

"Thank the Lord," I said to myself. "The Lord is working."

A businessman living near the home where I was staying attended regularly, and one night at 11:00 PM, he called me to his home, where I had the joy of leading him to Christ. Sometime later, his wife was saved. We were all overjoyed at this, but none of us realized what an important role this would have in connection with our moving to Marion. Later, when this couple decided to sell their home, a nice brick cottage next door to my host, Silas Cummings, they offered it to brother Cummings at a most attractive price if he would rent it to us. Although he did not see his way clear to accept their offer, another family in the assembly bought it. While we were in Canada on a brief visit, they sent word that the assembly had rented it for us, and it would be ready for our occupancy. Once again God had provided a dwelling for us, this time a house, very suitable for our growing family. Our two fleeces were again wet with the dew of heaven. We gathered our few belongings in Bristol, told our landlady and dear friend "Nana McElrath" goodbye, and moved on November 12, 1937. What peace there is in being able to say, "I being in the way the Lord led me" (Gen. 24:27).

Settling into our new home in Marion, and enjoying happy fellowship with the local Christians, we continued our former busy schedule of activities: preaching the gospel in the tent, chapels, schools, open air, factories, and even in the state institution for the criminally insane. We also continued encouraging the five small assemblies in the area, and doing much visitation. An enthusiastic tract band was formed in Marion, meeting regularly to stuff tracts into envelopes attractively inscribed "Good News for You Within." They distributed far and wide, relying on the promise, "He that soweth bountifully shall reap also bountifully."

As we continued on in the school of God, daily seeking to learn the lessons, we increasingly realized that the path of service and spiritual fruitfulness for the Lord was a life of continual contrasts. It had its ups and downs. Israel was given an earthly inheritance of "hills and valleys" (Deut. 11:11). To God's heavenly people—the Church—the path of obedience is one of sunshine and shadow, testing and triumph, need and supply, a path that tests the faith, for "we walk by faith, not by sight." God's first concern is for the development of His workers, then for the progress of His work.

With added experience in the service of the Lord comes, among other things, increased sensitivity to the leading of the Lord and the ability to distinguish between the restlessness of the flesh and the stirring of the Spirit. Spiritual ears will recognize "the sound of a going in the top of the mulberry trees" (2 Sam. 5:24). As 1938 drew toward a close, both Gertie and I were convinced that the Lord had another move for us; but when and where we did not know, so we began praying again for discernment as to His leading.

The new year began with an invitation from the Toronto Central Assembly to join with W. G. Smith in a gospel campaign in the Bracondale Gospel Hall, the place where I had first taught a Sunday School class of boys. Although the winter was a very severe one in Canada, attendance at the eight weeks of meetings was remarkable. Starting small, the numbers soon passed the 200 mark. Often standing room was at a premium. It was a series saturated with prayer, and God graciously answered with "showers of blessing." Many of those saved were the children of Christian parents; they had heard the gospel many times, but were "gospel hardened." Deep conviction was wrought in them by the Spirit of God. Many nights it was in the small hours of the morning before I retired. Like many others, I was stricken with the flu, but continued to preach, sometimes with a temperature of over 100. On one such night, after preaching I was drenched with perspiration. Fearing I might take pneumonia, I slipped down a back stairway to dry off in the furnace room while brother Smith preached. To my surprise, the young daughter of a Christian couple left the meeting and sought me out there, so deeply convicted she could not wait until the service ended. What a joy to lead her to Christ in that unlikely surrounding! It was a grand start for the new year, a year that was to include one of my most important moves in the Lord's service.

On May 3, we received a visit from Lester Wilson, who had been laboring for the Lord in North Carolina. His meetings in the capital city of Raleigh, where there was a small assembly, and in nearby places, had been blessed of the Lord with many conversions. Moving to Winston Salem, he had held tent meetings for several summers. A good number of conversions had resulted, but in 1938, following a citywide campaign in a warehouse by Dr. Mordecai Ham, the windows of heaven had been opened, and brother Wilson's meetings were crowned with the salvation of many souls. Bible readings followed, many were baptized, the little assembly practically doubled in number, and a new chapel had been erected. Now brother Wilson, true pioneer that he was, felt exercised about beginning a work in Greensboro, 30 miles east of Winston Salem. But he realized that the little flock in Winston Salem needed much further shepherding, so he had come to urge me to move there for that purpose. We talked far into the night, and I told him about our growing conviction that the Lord had an imminent move for us. It was decided that I go to Winston Salem and look over the situation. I left on the 13th and began a week of meetings in the chapel the next day.

What followed belongs in the next chapter on North Carolina, but I might add here that 1939, which had begun so auspiciously with the outpouring of blessing on the meetings in Toronto, ended on a similar note in the same city, at the Swanwick Gospel Hall. After prayerful consideration, I felt the Lord was leading me to accept an invitation to hold a series of gospel meetings in that assembly. Although there were some very fine believers there, a season of drought in conversion had created almost a spirit of pessimism. It was rather stiff at first, but persistence, prayer, and preaching of the Word turned the tide. Attendance increased, and soon the prayer sessions were larger than the gospel meetings had been at the beginning. Then God's Spirit began a work of deep conviction in many unsaved, and not only I but many of the elders were kept busy night after night in the grand occupation of pointing souls to Christ. It was a glorious conclusion to a good year.

Harold G. Mackay shortly before surgery in 1964

JOHN & AGNES MACKAY
(H. G.'S PARENTS) ON THEIR
50TH WEDDING ANNIVERSARY

IN THE WINTER OF 1926-27,
H. G. MACKAY WORKING
AS A LOGGER

LATE SUMMER, 1926 ON THE MANITOBA HARVEST EXCURSION

THE FAMILY HOME ON SOUTH STREET IN GALT, ONTARIO

THE AINSLEE STREET GOSPEL HALL, GALT, ONTARIO,
THE SPIRITUAL BIRTHPLACE OF H. G. MACKAY ON MAY 23, 1926

WITH FRANK M. DETWEILER, OUR SMALL CAMPER
LIVING QUARTERS IN JOHNSON CITY, TENNESSEE

OUR TENT PITCHED IN PENNINGTON GAP, VIRGINIA

THE TENT-TABERNACLE NEAR ASHEVILLE, NORTH CAROLINA IN 1928

JAMES LYON, H. G. MACKAY'S FIRST CO-LABORER IN THE GOSPEL

WITH WM. GILLESPIE, SR. IN OSHAWA, ON. IN 1928

WITH WM. GILLESPIE, JR. IN PITTSBURGH, PA. IN 1930

WEDDING DAY FOR GERTRUDE AND HAROLD MACKAY
NOVEMBER 25, 1931

HAROLD & GERTRUDE
C. 1970

AT WINSTON-SALEM,
NORTH CAROLINA
WITH JACK AND STAN

THE FAMILY AT THE MACKAY'S SIXTIETH WEDDING ANNIVERSARY
NOVEMBER 25, 1991

W. G. and Ruth
Smith, fellow-
workers in
West Virginia
and North
Carolina

Mr. & Mrs.
Mackay with
Lester Wilson
at the
celebration of
50 years in the
Lord's work

The Mackay
home at 2512
W. Vandalia
Road in
Greensboro for
forty years.

8
Settled in North Carolina

I can use the term "settled" now in retrospect, but when I made my first visit to North Carolina in 1928 with William Gillespie, Sr., I had no idea that the major part of my service for the Lord would be in that state. Nor, when we moved to North Carolina in 1939, did I imagine that we would be located here for over half a century. But so it has proved to be. The "trial week" of meetings in the chapel at Winston Salem seemed to bear the stamp of the Lord's approval; I was warmly received by the Christians, attendance increased nightly, and we heard of at least one person trusting Christ. The second fleece we had put out was also wet with tokens of divine guidance. Unexpectedly, through unusual circumstances, the house next door to the chapel on Glenn Avenue became available for rent. Although it was not in the best condition, I felt it was the Lord's place for us, so I returned to Marion to get Gertie, the boys, and our furnishings.

Once we were settled into the house in Winston Salem, I pitched my tent in two locations that summer: Montview, a suburb of the city, and, later, on one of the city's busy thoroughfares. The Lord graciously blessed the preaching of His gospel and souls were saved, even though it was a season of severe electrical storms and on several occasions the tent was badly damaged, necessitating extensive repairs. On October 1, two baptismal services were held in the Glenn Avenue Chapel, twelve converts being baptized in the afternoon session and eleven at the evening one. It was an encouraging commencement of our labors for the Lord in North Carolina.

I began to realize what an important preparatory period the years in West Virginia and Virginia had been. In Winston Salem there was much to be done and many opportunities to put into practice the experience I had gained. Like Solomon's workmen, brother Wilson had hewed out of the rock of nature stones for the assembly (1 Ki. 5:17); now these needed the work of the stonesquarers (1 Ki. 5:18).

One of my first priorities was the large and growing Sunday School. I began to set up special training classes for those who wished to teach. Then I prepared a series of lessons, mimeographing the lesson for each class. This entailed many hours of work, but I enjoyed it to the full. Eventually, as the growth continued, additional space for the classes became necessary. An attractive little chapel had been built on Glenn Avenue, but no special provision had been made for Sunday School rooms. It was not feasible to add on a classroom wing. Where would we find space?

There was only one answer—under the chapel. Only enough basement space had been excavated to house the heating equipment, so I began digging out space for the Sunday School rooms, soon joined by other brethren. This was truly a work of faith, because I knew that the Chapel's finances could not possibly stretch to cover the materials needed to construct and furnish the rooms. Gertie and I prayed, and we decided to take a further personal step of faith: we told the brethren that we would not accept any monetary fellowship from the assembly until the Sunday School rooms were completed. As He always does, the Lord continued to meet our financial needs in other ways, and in time we had our sorely-needed rooms completed and ready for occupancy.

If it was a full life, it was a happy and fruitful one: souls were being saved, attendance at the services was increasing, the believers were maturing spiritually, and the influence of the assembly was extending in ever-widening circles. The weekly remembrance of our Lord at His table was a most precious time of worship, as delightful as I have ever experienced, and seven days seemed too long from Lord's Day to Lord's Day. Not that we were exempt from trials— by no means! There were plenty of them: health, satanic attacks of discouragement, finances. Our total income for the year was a little less than $2,000. Of course, a dollar went a lot further then.

Our next year followed much the same pattern. The chapel services were well attended with some conversions. The local brethren increasingly participated in the worship at the Lord's Supper, and a few gave evidence of gift and began to minister in a limited way. We began a library with helpful books for both adults and senior Sunday School students. A tract band faithfully covered the neighborhood of the chapel with invitations and literature. Tent meetings were held in various locations in the city, but again severe storms damaged the tent, this time rendering it unfit for use. In Greensboro, brother Wilson had designed and constructed a portable tabernacle with substantial wooden framework and a canvas covering. I purchased this and pitched it in Winston Salem. From the first, there was excellent attendance, souls began to be saved, including three young sisters in one family, who became bright witnesses for the Lord, resulting in the conversion of their mother.

The Easter weekend of 1941 was the occasion of what was to become an annual event for over 40 years—the Piedmont Easter Bible Conference. Convened in the newly-purchased Forest Avenue Tabernacle in Greensboro, it was attended by more than 300. Refreshing and edifying ministry was given by Robert Crawford, John Bramhall, and Harold Harper. My diary for April 12, reads: "In the afternoon took a carload to Greensboro. Nice number present. Robert Crawford spoke on 'Christ Is All,' Brother Harper on 'The Man of Thy Right Hand.' Good keynotes for the conference."

I had assumed the responsibility for organizing the food service, with each of the three area assemblies—Raleigh, Winston Salem, and Greensboro—providing the food for one day . As a result, I found it necessary to miss many of the services. Meals were served on two levels of the building, and many a leg ache reminded local Christians of the conference! Yet, as Lester Wilson wrote, "It was something never to be forgotten," and my diary for April 14 says, "God has exceeded our expectations!" It is difficult even for those of us who were in the midst of it to recapture the thrill of that first Piedmont conference. There was a freshness and fervor about it that more than compensated for the strenuous labor.

If possible, 1942 held even a busier schedule for me than the previous years. With the increased attendance at the assembly came greater demands upon time and strength for visitation, counselling, preaching and teaching, and for the instruction of speakers, Sunday School teachers, youth workers, leaders. When the tent/tabernacle was taken out of winter storage, not only did it need repairs from the damage of the previous season's storms, but also from damage done by a fire in the storage area. But in due time it was erected on the south side of the city, and nightly meetings commenced. The radio program moved to a new early morning time, three days a week at 6:45 AM, thus reaching many who were commuting to their work in the city from neighboring localities. Improvements were made on the chapel, both exterior and interior, and I quickly learned that the best way to enlist willing workers was to get one's own hands busy and dirty. There is little room in the Lord's harvest fields for "gentleman farmers."

In Greensboro the Lord had blessed the preaching of Brother Wilson; a good number had been saved, baptized, and were being taught New Testament church truths. The Forest Avenue Tabernacle now housed a small but thriving assembly testimony. Lester was traveling more, however, and it therefore fell on me to assist in the work there, particularly after he felt led of the Lord to begin nightly services in Burlington, about twenty miles east of Greensboro. Mr. and Mrs. Ernest Gross, who had been helping him in the music and children's work, moved to Graham, near Burlington, and I found myself conducting two other morning broadcasts, one in Greensboro and one in Burlington.

Recognizing that this could not continue indefinitely, we spent much time in prayerful consultation. Was it the Lord's time for me to move to Greensboro? In August, I moved the tent/tabernacle there and erected it on a rented lot on Elam Avenue. Meetings began with a good earnest, and I began searching for a suitable house to rent. However, a diligent search produced only one prospect, which, while attractive from a financial aspect, was in a very fashionable section of the city. Gertie and I both felt uneasy about that, since it did not seem compatible with the work I would be doing. A terrific storm left the canvas top of the tabernacle in shreds, so that it had to be dismantled and the meetings discontinued. Was God trying to tell us something?

There were others that we wondered if the Lord might be preparing for this work. Robert Halliday was holding meetings in various places nearby; W. G. Smith was giving help from time to time; Brother Wilson was in contact with a young man, William Brown, who had been commended to the Lord's work by his home assembly in Patterson, New Jersey, and who was exercised about coming to North Carolina. Pray and plan as we might, there seemed to be no clear indication of the will of God for our moving. Finally, I became convinced that the time had not yet come for us to locate in Greensboro. God was saying: "Stand still and see" (Ex. 14:13); in His own time He would say: "Go forward!" (v. 15). And so it proved.

As had been the case in Winston Salem, Brother Wilson found that his final year in Greensboro was the most fruitful; many were saved and baptized, and the newly acquired chapel gave a much more stable character to the assembly testimony. In January of 1943, the Brown family moved from New Jersey to Greensboro, and Bill was soon involved in the various phases of the work, while Brother Wilson turned his main attention to the new effort in Burlington.

The year 1943 began with a week of meetings at the Raleigh chapel. I also spoke each morning that week on Tommy Steele's radio program on the powerful radio station WPTF and had a Bible reading afterward with the radio staff. There was a keen interest in these studies, and Tommy was led later to cast in his lot with the assemblies, in which he has enjoyed happy fellowship and carried on a fruitful ministry ever since. His son Tommy Jr. has followed in his footsteps. [Ed. note: Tommy Steele, Sr. went to be with the Lord in May 1993, only two weeks after Mr. Mackay's homecall.]

In Winston Salem I rented a vacant building near the site of the tent meetings of 1942. Having stood empty for some time, its many windows had proved tempting targets for the neighborhood boys, so that there was not an unbroken one in the entire building. Brother Binkley procured the use of a fire department pump and the building received its first bath in many years. Broken glass was patiently chipped out and paint began to transform the building's appearance. A large attractive sign GOSPEL SERVICES indicated to passersby the purpose of the renovated building, and each week the neighborhood was covered with announcements of the services. Meetings for children and an hour later for adults were held nightly. From the opening night there was encouraging interest and attendance; the 200 chairs that brother Cromer had borrowed from the city were frequently all occupied, with more being needed at times. Some fine trophies of grace were won to the Saviour in that building.

Although the Lord thus placed His stamp of approval on our remaining in Winston Salem for the time, a new train of events was underway that showed His encouragement to us to prepare for another move. William Brown moved from Greensboro to Asheville in August of 1943, leaving much of the responsibility on me to assist in the radio and assembly ministry in Greensboro. When brother Wilson was out of the state, this also included the new assembly in Burlington, where there was a third radio broadcast.

Once again the question faced us: "Is it the Lord's will for us to move to Greensboro?" From there we could more conveniently assist Winston to the west and Burlington to the east. As in the past, when faced with this important decision, we put before the Lord the fleece of finding suitable living quarters. Although wartime restrictions had created a scarcity in rental property, in contrast to our past failures we quickly located a newly renovated house just two doors from the Forest Avenue Tabernacle where the assembly met. On November 4, 1943, we moved to 622 Forest Street, not aware that Greensboro would be our home for nearly fifty years.

9
Building on the Foundation

"[Paul] planted, Apollos watered, but God gave the increase" *(1 Cor. 3:6).*

On June 6, 1939, two young Canadian evangelists entered the office of Police Chief Jarvis in the city of Greensboro, North Carolina. One of them, Lester Wilson, recorded the ensuing encounter:

I said, "Chief Jarvis, I want to have some meetings in this city, but I understand there is a by-law prohibiting the erection of a tent inside the city limits, and I use a tent for my services."

"Yes," he said, "there is such an ordinance. What do you preach—Christ and Him crucified?"

I said, "Yes, and risen, glorified, and coming again!"

His reply was a fervent "Amen!"

I was the other evangelist. Chief Jarvis sent us with his recommendation to Mayor Lewis and the aldermen, who in turn advised that we get permission from the Ministerial Association. The president of that group said, "I don't see any reason why we can't let you go ahead. We don't want to be the only ones blocking you. It's all right with us."

Lester Wilson's first Greensboro campaign started on June 18, 1939, with the tent pitched on Wharton Street, just two lots from the home of Chief Jarvis. Another campaign followed in August with the tent pitched on Eugene Street. Attendance grew from 45 at the first meeting to about 150 before the campaign closed on October 3.

Many professed to be saved during that summer, and many other fine local Christians were soon attracted to the enthusiastic group of believers that thus began to grow. During the winter months, a series of Bible studies kept the group together until the spring of 1940, when the tent was again erected, this time behind the YMCA on Sycamore Street.

Lester recorded in his journal, "On May 9, I first heard of a church building for sale on Forest Street." It had now become apparent that the Divine Builder was providing the stones for a New Testament assembly in Greensboro, and a permanent building was needed to house the testimony and carry on the work. On July 26, Brother Wilson and Raymond Schuster, who had come to help with the music and the children's services, went to look at the former Forest Avenue Baptist Church. As they sat in the car looking at the building, a man came walking up the street, looked at the car, and walked slowly by. When he was about twenty feet past the car, he stopped, turned around, and came back. He said, "Are you the preacher that is interested in this church?" He went on to tell brother Wilson that he had attended the tent meeting and liked what he heard. "I hope you get the building," he said.

This stranger was a strong local Christian, W. B. Andrews, Sr., and this contact would have far-reaching effects on the work. Lester Wilson's journal records the result:

"Mr. Andrews put us in contact with a Dr. Battle, who was the chairman of the building committee in the Baptist congregation that owned the building. An agreement was reached; the building was purchased for $5,000, with an additional $200 for the pews. No payment was to be made on the $5,000 until December. This gave time for the necessary renovation to be made, as it was in a run-down condition. Brother Andrews volunteered to do the necessary painting (he was a painting contractor); new windows were installed, and some carpeting was put down. Rubbish was cleared out of the basement, and the furnace was put in running order. The first service held in it was a Bible study on September 25, with fifty present. In October, a schedule of regular services was begun, with 45 in the Sunday School, 90 at 11:00 AM, and 125 at the night service on the opening day."

This building became known as the Forest Avenue Tabernacle, reflecting its origins in Lester Wilson's wooden and canvas tent-tabernacle. It continued to be the gathering place of the Greensboro assembly until 1967, when the new Shannon Hills Chapel was built. It was a real step of faith for the infant assembly to assume in 1940 the obligation of the $5,000 mortgage, but after four years a brother in the Lord offered an interest-free loan of $3,700 to clear off the mortgage. This loan was completely repaid by December of 1945.

One other important development in Greensboro needs to be discussed here—instituting the now-common Family Bible Hour. As the young assembly began to grow in its new home, its schedule of services included Sunday School and preaching, but brother Wilson had not yet introduced the breaking of bread service. More spiritual maturity was necessary before the local Christians would be able to support effectively the worship characteristic of that service. Lester thus drove to Winston Salem to meet with the assembly there for the weekly remembrance of the Lord.

When it seemed that the appropriate time had come for the Lord's Supper to be included in the schedule of services at the Tabernacle, the problem was to find a suitable time. Many unsaved people were attending the 11:00 service; it would be difficult for them to understand their exclusion from the Lord's Supper. Others were professing Christians who gave very little evidence of being truly born again. The Lord's Supper could not be opened to all, saved and unsaved. What was the solution to the problem?

Brother Wilson and I prayed much together about this, as well as consulting with others. The solution began at the first Easter Conference in Greensboro in April of 1941. By now the local Christians had learned much about New Testament assembly principles. At that wonderful conference, many of them experienced for the first time the joy of breaking bread, surrounded by 225 like-minded believers. On the Sunday following the Easter Conference, the Greensboro assembly had their first Remembrance Feast, scheduled in the afternoon in order to have the usual Sunday School and preaching services in the morning. I brought two carloads of Christians over from Winston Salem to join them and to help participate in the worship.

It was clear, however, that the afternoon was not going to be an effective time for the Lord's Supper. The Greensboro Christians thus decided to remember the Lord on Sunday mornings at 9:45, and follow this with a combined Sunday School and preaching service at 11:00 AM, which they called the "Family Bible Hour." This was the first time the Family Bible Hour was established in the South, to our knowledge. This change continues to this day, and has now spread through practically all the assemblies in the South, as well as many others throughout the United States.

It was to this assembly gathering in Greensboro's Forest Avenue Tabernacle that the Lord led us in November of 1943. I had been integrally involved with Brother Wilson in each step of establishing this work, so we already felt at home here. Although we had the complete assurance that the Lord was leading us to Greensboro, it was not easy to leave Winston Salem where we had many spiritual children, and where many facets of the testimony we had implemented were beginning to bear fruit.

Meanwhile Lester had established a small assembly in Burlington, soon followed by others in Durham, Siler City, and Sanford. One of my first concerns in all of this burgeoning new life was to maintain a unified effort among these six groups. Furthermore, after the United States' entry into World War II, many assembly Christians were being drafted for military service, and we felt the need of keeping them informed of assembly activities as well as giving them helpful ministry from the Word. To meet both of these objectives, we decided to publish a newsletter to be called *The Piedmont Assembly Messenger.* One of brother W. B. Andrews' sons, Dick, took a leading role in this project, assisted by Miss Lois Fitch. The initial issue came out in December 1943. I contributed the lead article, "Thou Crownest the Year with Thy Goodness." There were also reports from Burlington, Greensboro, Raleigh, Siler City, and Winston Salem, and articles on youth work, the radio ministry, address changes, coming meetings, prayer requests, and servicemen's news.

This little paper continued for a number of years, contributing much to establishing the Lord's work in the Piedmont.

After planting these six assemblies in North Carolina, Lester Wilson eventually located in Albany, Georgia. As the work in the Piedmont area of North Carolina developed, the Lord brought a number of His servants to labor there. There was, of course, an interchange of ministry and the development of local gift. Ernie Gross helped in the Burlington area before eventually moving on to South Carolina. Bill Brown moved to Asheville, then to Florida. Gordon Reager and William Bousfield both assisted in the work in Winston Salem before moving out of state. W. G. Smith moved to Burlington, remaining there until his homecall. Welcome Detweiler continues to reside in Durham where he has had a most fruitful ministry. It reminded me of 2 Timothy 4:10-12, where the Apostle Paul speaks of those who later served the Lord in local churches he had planted in eastern Europe and Asia Minor. (Ed. note: Mr. Detweiler went to be with the Lord in April 1992, having preached on the preceding Sunday. He was followed in November of that year by Lester Wilson, who spent his last years in the Pittsboro Christian Village.]

Gertie and I, with our sons, soon found ourselves settled in the boxy white two-story house two doors up from the Tabernacle, enjoying happy fellowship with the local believers. Our home was an accessible haven for lonely servicemen stationed at the Overseas Replacement Depot (ORD) camp which had been established in Greensboro, and many took advantage of the standing invitation. Gertie's motherly hospitality and obvious concern for them touched their hearts. She often decorated our living room with flowers and baked a cake for some of their weddings, at which they had asked me to officiate. The family atmosphere was a welcome relief for many of these homesick young men, and we never knew who we might find on the couch or floor of our living room when we opened the bedroom door in the morning. A window opening onto the front porch was a favorite means of entry for latecomers after the family had gone to sleep.

Many Christian servicemen, from assemblies and independent

churches throughout the country, found a warm welcome and fellowship awaiting them at the Tabernacle. They often sent word to their wives and fiancees that they too were welcome, and many visits resulted, bringing cheer to the hearts of those facing the trial of separation from loved ones. There were few Lord's Days during the war years that did not witness soldiers, and often their wives, seated at the hospitable tables of Greensboro assembly Christians.

These Christian soldiers often brought their unsaved buddies to the Tabernacle so that many came to know the Lord through the testimony there. They even included the reputed "toughest top sergeant in the camp," whose heart was nevertheless softened by the saving gospel. Another memorable convert was the mess sergeant, who kept the Christian hostesses posted on the camp menu, so that they could arrange to serve a welcome change from Army fare!

We will perhaps never know in this life all of the fruit from the assembly care for these servicemen, but a letter received by a local sister in 1975 gives a hint of some of the glad surprises that may be in store at a coming day of review and revelation. A chaplain (colonel) in the United States Army wrote:

"I was a young soldier in 1945. I had been in the army for over two years at the time and my concern about where I was in relation to God had reached a critical point. I particularly remember my utter spiritual confusion—almost despair—one Sunday morning while stationed at Greensboro Army Air Corps Base. For many months I had been bouncing back and forth between confidence that I was a Christian, and the uncertainty as to whether I was or not. That particular Sunday morning I had very successfully utilized the Communion—the Lord's Supper. I'd participated in the Remembrance Feast at the Base Chapel that morning. I felt pretty good about myself and my assurance was high. Later on that day, however, in listening to a radio broadcast of a church service, my sense of well-being and spiritual security vanished. The contrast between the two states was so great, and so discouraging, that I knew I had to get this resolved, finally. Although I was a member of another denomination, I decided to attend the Greensboro assembly. (I had

visited assemblies in other places, along with many other denominational churches, and I knew that a clear gospel message would be
presented.) I took a bus to the chapel; Mr. Mackay was the preacher, and I wasn't disappointed. That night the Good News of God's
love was simply, clearly presented. I accepted God's promise hun-
grily, almost desperately. For over a year I had been in spiritual tur-
moil, longing for an assurance of being a child of God that would
not be wafted away on the first wind of doubt. But from that day
I've been sure of God's love and unchanging grace, and my relationship to Him. . . . My present assignment is as Deputy Comman-
dant for Training and Education at the Army Chaplain Center and
School. This means that I am responsible for the resident training of
all chaplains (basic and advanced) and all chaplain assistants."

How many more were saved and blessed during the war years we
will not know until the Judgment Seat of Christ.

With all of this growth, there came increased demands on our
time. When I was able to get out of state for a brief change, it was to
minister at a conference, teach at Emmaus Bible School, or conduct
a series of nightly meetings at an assembly. There were five radio
broadcasts associated with the area assemblies, and always births,
sicknesses, weddings, and funerals, all demanding much time and
attention. The Lord seemed to be making it clear to us that the days
of our pioneer work were over; there were now constant needs to be
met in our immediate area. For the first time, I entertained the idea
that perhaps the Lord intended me to stay on in Greensboro indefinitely as a resident worker.

It is obviously crucial to guard against a ministry leading to an
unscriptural clergy-laity distinction in the assemblies. Many local
assemblies, however, have been stunted in infancy by being left
without the care of an experienced shepherd. Too much responsibility, either in leadership or ministry, or both, has been thrust on immature believers, with disastrous results. With all his faults, Jacob
was a wise shepherd, and his words to Esau might profitably be
pondered by all those entrusted with the pastoral care of a young assembly: "And he said to him, My lord knoweth that the children are

77

tender, and the flocks and herds with young are with me, and if men overdrive them one day, all the flock will die. Let my lord, I pray thee, pass over before his servant, and I will lead on softly according as the cattle that goeth before me and the children be able to bear" (Gen. 33:13-14).

During these early years of "watering" the Greensboro assembly "planted" by brother Wilson, I began to research the subject of elders and the oversight, presenting my findings to the Christians. It is quite clear that the teaching of the New Testament is that Spirit-made elders (Acts 20:28) are the guides, or leaders, of the local assembly, and as such are to be recognized and obeyed (Heb. 13:7, 17, 24). Yet these are not over-lords, but under-shepherds (1 Pet. 5:3-4). The governing body in the local assembly is the elderhood, the oversight, the "presbytery" as it is called in 1 Timothy 4:14. This latter Scripture clearly indicates that there were not only individual elders in the early church, who shepherded the flock, but an oversight of such elders who acted in conjunction as the representatives of the local assembly.

In the early days of an assembly, the pioneer preacher must provide much, if not all, of the leadership. But this is a temporary situation, and he should faithfully instruct the Lord's people in the New Testament truth concerning elders and the oversight, meanwhile praying that the Chief Shepherd will raise up true shepherds to "take the oversight" (1 Pet. 5:1-6). This was done in Greensboro, with the result that by 1947, the consensus of opinion was that the time had come for a definitely recognized oversight. Ministry had been given on the subject, and much prayer went up to God for definite guidance in this important step.

The Greensboro Christians carefully examined the scriptural qualifications for these spiritual leaders as set forth in 1 Timothy 3:1-6 and Titus 1:6-9. It was agreed that no *perfect* elders might be expected; nevertheless the basic requirements of godliness, sound judgment, spiritual maturity, and a good testimony both within and outside the assembly, seemed absolutely requisite.

The question now arose: "How should such be recognized?" Certainly nothing in the Scriptures indicated an election by the brethren or by the whole assembly. There are now no apostles to ordain elders (Acts 14:23), nor apostolic delegates such as Titus (Titus 1:5). And yet the detailed instructions in Paul's closing epistles (Timothy and Titus) strongly infer that elders are to continue throughout the church age, even after the apostles are gone. Should the absence of specific instructions as to the proper procedure for recognizing them prevent the local assembly from recognizing their spiritual guides, especially since the spiritual qualifications were given in the Word? The Greensboro brethren were persuaded that they could depend on the Holy Spirit to guide them in this matter of recognizing elders after prayerfully committing it to Him.

And so, on May 26, 1947, a meeting of all the brethren in the fellowship was convened at the Forest Avenue Tabernacle for the purpose of definitely recognizing the God-given elders in the assembly. Looking back after more than 40 years, it is abundantly evident that this meeting was of God, and that it was to have a tremendous influence and beneficial effect on the future of the assembly. It began with a session of prayer, and a spirit of reverential awe and total dependence on God pervaded the entire service. It was decided that each brother who so desired would be at liberty to state whom he believed was qualified to assume the solemn responsibility of being a guide in the assembly. When a name was mentioned, that brother was asked to leave the room while his qualifications (or lack of them) were frankly, but graciously, discussed. It was a meeting never to be forgotten by those present.

Those who were finally decided upon were queried as to their personal exercise before the Lord in regard to this responsible ministry. Without exception, each one expressed a sense of inadequacy and unworthiness, and yet of appreciation for the confidence manifested by his brethren, and a sincere desire to please the Lord and serve His people. Those who were recognized at that time, and who thus composed the original oversight of the Forest Avenue Tabernacle, were P. S. Alley, W. B. Andrews, Sr., C. R. (Dick) Andrews, Ben Coble, Voight Everhart, W. E. Gardner, H. G. Mackay, Paul

Tuttle, and J. B. Westmoreland. The Greensboro assembly profited and grew under the guidance of these men.

For five years we continued to live at 622 Forest Street, our proximity to the Tabernacle bringing many visitors to our door for brief or more protracted visits. During this time, our third son, Ron, was born, and with our active two older boys, we began to feel the need of more space for the family. In 1948, we found a brick house shaded by beautiful oaks and dogwoods on the outskirts of the city, but easily accessible to the Tabernacle by a good suburban bus system as well as by car. Although the house had only five rooms, there was an unfinished attic that we were able to develop into bedrooms and a small bath for the boys. Here there would be a greater degree of privacy, increasingly needed for my personal study time, as well as a place for our growing sons to climb trees and make forts in the wooded area behind our home. We were also able to plant a small vegetable garden, and Gertie enjoyed transplanting wild flowers and the cuttings given to her by friends in the assembly. Our yard was often the scene of youth socials and picnics for the Christians. This has remained our home throughout our years of service.

(Ed. note: Because of failing health, the Mackays moved to the Pittsboro Christian Village retirement center in March of 1992, where they found happy fellowship until Mr. Mackay's homecall in April of 1993. As of this printing, Mrs. Mackay still lives there, surrounded by many friends developed throughout their labors together.)

10
Ever-Widening Circles

"A fruitful bough by a well, whose branches run over the wall"
(Gen. 49:22).

The patriarch Jacob described his beloved son Joseph in these words, but they seem applicable to the Greensboro assembly during the 1950's. It was a joy to watch the steady spiritual growth of this young body of believers, both individually and collectively. The evangelizing emphasis of the 1930's and '40's and the emotional upheaval of the war years slowly mellowed into the serenity and desire for stability of the '50's. Under the shepherd-care of the elders, Forest Avenue Tabernacle continued to solidify, adding a vital youth ministry, strengthening the Sunday School, encouraging Bible study through both home and assembly groups. As its own roots thus ran deeper into the well of God's Word, its branches began to spread beyond the local gathering into the community and into collective efforts of the regional assemblies.

The late 1940's and early '50's continued to be busy ones for me, both in Greensboro and in responsibilities elsewhere. One particularly enjoyable role from 1947 through 1952 was that of visiting instructor at the Emmaus Bible School (now Emmaus Bible College in Dubuque, Iowa) in both of its early locations, Toronto and Chicago. One of the advantages of a long life is the opportunity it affords of personally observing the development of an influential movement, in this case Emmaus, from its modest inception to an extensive sphere. Early in my Christian life in Toronto, I met J. R. Littleproud, a devout believer, an elder in the Swanwick Avenue assembly, and a gifted Bible teacher and author. Deeply concerned about the spiritual development of young men and women, he began an evening Bible class which was well attended and was a beneficial influence on many lives. This was one of several small seeds from which the Emmaus Bible School developed.

From the beginning, Emmaus had a dual faculty system: a strong resident faculty, which would give stability and continuity to the program; and visiting instructors, men who were busily engaged in the Lord's work in various fields of service. These would add variety and contemporary experience, enabling the students to profit from their contact with real-life characteristics, problems, and opportunities.

In 1947, I was invited to become a member of the visiting faculty; I taught at intervals in Toronto through 1952 and at the Chicago campus from 1948-1950. It was a challenging and rewarding experience to instruct the splendid young men and women in the student body. Most, if not all, were mature beyond their years in attitude and aspirations. Many of the male students had seen active duty overseas during World War II; they had seen life and death in its reality. They had also seen firsthand the need in other lands and had come home determined to take full advantage of their Christian opportunities. The girls were of equally fine calibre. I enjoyed these classes to the full; these young people stretched me intellectually and spiritually as much as I did them. Today I see many of their names in connection with the work of the Lord here and abroad, and I rejoice and pray for them.

In 1949, while teaching at the school in Chicago, I was invited to conduct the Moody Bible Institute's *Bread of Life* program, aired over their two radio stations WMBI and WDLM. This program was preceded and followed by a half-hour of music, leaving a full thirty-minute segment of uninterrupted Bible study. For one week, I gave studies on "The Life of Elijah, the Prophet of God."

This led to an invitation for me to participate in January of 1950 at the Moody Founder's Week Conference, sponsored by the Moody Bible Institute of Chicago. The evening services were held in the spacious Moody Memorial Church, drawing audiences of up to 5,000, with outstanding speakers from this country and others. The morning services, held at the Institute, were smaller, attended mainly by students and fundamental preachers from many parts of the country. I was asked to share in the Bible teaching at the morning sessions. I did so, ministering on the book of Ruth, "From Failure to Fruitfulness." These studies were also aired on the Institute's radio stations, drawing many requests for copies of their outlines.

In addition to my stints as visiting instructor at Emmaus, I had another enjoyable group of experiences with teaching young people at the Guelph Summer Bible School from 1947 through 1951. This was a combined camp, conference, youth retreat, and Bible school. The School was held on the grounds of the Guelph Bible Conference, the majority of the young people housed in cabins with mature leaders, frequently missionaries home on furlough. This made a strong missionary impression on the students, resulting in much exercise about service in foreign fields.

In 1950, in response to numerous invitations, I made my first visit to California, on the way visiting the Good News Center in New Orleans during a stopover for a change of trains. In Los Angeles, I assisted in the Vacation Bible School at La Brea Chapel, giving daily lessons illustrated by beautiful hand-painted felts, and telling missionary stories. The lessons drew a gathering of Catholic children, who were forbidden by their parents to enter the chapel, but they stood at a side entrance and listened intently.

I visited several other California assemblies and went on to speak at the Forest Home Camp, where over 300 children were assembled for two weeks of camp. My visit there was abruptly terminated, however, when Gertie phoned that my mother was in critical condition. I flew to her bedside in Galt, finding her very weak and in an oxygen tent. Slowly she began to recover. Once she was out of danger, I returned home to Greensboro.

I was able to return to the West Coast in 1951 for another week at the Forest Home Camp and a week at the Yosemite Conference. While other summer conferences may be defined as a Bible conference with a vacation included, Yosemite is a vacation with a conference included. No special accommodations for united lodging or meals are available, guests being responsible for their own. Because of the breathtaking natural beauty of the valley, sightseeing takes the place of organized recreation. For one unforgettable week I shared the ministry with Richard Hill and Peter Pell, having the joy of seeing several profess faith in the Lord.

One of the most fruitful outreaches of the work in Greensboro for nearly 40 years was the radio ministry. When Lester Wilson pitched his gospel tent here in 1939, he was a total stranger to the people of Greensboro. He realized that one of his first needs was to acquaint them with the nature of the meetings he was going to conduct and the message he was going to preach. The unsavory conduct of some tent-preachers who had preceded him in the city made this doubly imperative. Convinced that he could best accomplish this by means of radio broadcasts, he approached the manager of the local CBS affiliate, WBIG—"The Prestige Station of the Carolinas," as it proudly advertised itself. A contract was agreed upon, with payment to be made in advance weekly.

The Lord quickly honored this step of faith. A local woman who had attended the tent meetings was impressed by the complete absence of appeals for money, in contrast with the practice of other meetings she had been attending. She approached Lester Wilson one day and told him how she had just been ready to give her offering in response to a local church's appeal. She said, "Three or four times I just about put up my hand and something said, 'Don't you do it.' The Lord kept bringing you before me. I don't know where you get your money, but I just wondered if you would accept some fellowship from me. It's my tithe, and I don't know why I've let this accumulate." With that, she handed him a check for $250! Lester writes: "I walked right over to the station and paid it on the radio bill, so I was paid up for quite a while."

When Gertie and I moved to Greensboro, we assumed the financial responsibility for the broadcasts, as brother Wilson had done, since the assembly was small and struggling to pay off its mortgage.

Often grocery money was transferred to this account, so Gertie had to use even more ingenuity in preparing meals for the family and the many visitors who dropped in. (She still smiles about the number of people who asked her for recipes for dishes she had prepared from leftovers or odds and ends of food people had given us from their gardens.) But God in faithfulness met the needs, and the broadcasts continued in this way until the assembly was able to assume this obligation. For many years, two sisters went to the station with me to assist with the music: Alyce Ageon as soloist and Lib Gallimore (later Mrs. William Atkinson) as pianist.

The broadcasts were increased from two to four weekly, until in 1949 we settled on a half-hour program at 8:30 each Sunday morning, known as *Your Bible Says*. By the 1970's, this had become the oldest consecutive religious program on the air in Greensboro. Many visited the assembly as a result of hearing the broadcasts, and many other interesting personal contacts stemmed from it.

I once received a letter from a sailor stationed on a naval vessel in the Mediterranean, who insisted he had picked up the broadcast there. The station personnel explained this odd occurrence as a "stray" airwave that sometimes travels far beyond the normal reach of the station. I prefer to believe that it was "directed" by the God who controls the airwaves as well as the waves of the sea. Another memorable event that showed me the extent of this outreach occurred one night when I hurried to the hospital to comfort a young couple in the assembly, as the wife had just given birth to a stillborn baby. I was told I could not be admitted to the maternity section at that hour. Explaining the circumstances, I hurried to the elevator with a prayer for the Lord's assistance. A doctor was on the elevator pushing the buttons. Hearing my request for the maternity floor, he said over his shoulder, "An expectant father, I assume?"

"No," I said, "but I suppose I've visited as many new mothers as most doctors in this city."

"H. G. Mackay," he said, without looking around. "Your Canadian accent identified you. I listen to your broadcast regularly. Thank you."

85

With him as my official escort, the nurses asked no questions when I entered the room of the young mother.

Another productive and far-reaching local effort for the Forest Avenue Tabernacle was the 1951 Billy Graham Crusade at the Greensboro fairgrounds. Graham was just becoming nationally known, and friend and foe alike were uncertain as to his future. An important decision had to be reached regarding my personal course and that of the assembly in connection with the Crusade. I met with the elders frequently for prayer and consultation. Several options were considered before the Lord: Should we oppose it? Should we stand aloof from it? Should we publicly endorse it and cooperate? Should we adopt a neutral stance, with individual Christians being left free to follow their own conscience in the matter?

The problem could be viewed in quite a different light today, but then it was complex. I realized that some of the practices of the Crusade would be contrary to those of the assembly; some of the local leaders were ones who had been most vocal in their criticism and opposition to me; there would be many denominations with varied doctrines associated with the Crusade. On the other hand, to oppose it or even to stand aloof from it would be, in appearance at least, to be aligned with the Catholics (this was before they sanctioned the Crusades), the Unitarians, the Seventh Day Adventists, and the Jehovah's Witnesses. Not an enviable alignment indeed! I decided to cooperate just as much as I could without compromising my convictions or condoning what I had previously condemned. The elders decided to follow the same course.

Crusade preparations included two activities which immediately met the approval of the assembly Christians and won their participation. Ladies' neighborhood prayer meetings in homes throughout the city found many assembly sisters among the regular attendants. And, profiting from some unfortunate experiences on the West Coast, Billy Graham and his associates had invited the Navigators to assume full responsibility for the after-service counseling of those who responded to the invitation from the platform. Under the direction of Lorne Sanny, preparatory meetings were held for the careful screening of all counselors, every effort being made to ensure that they were truly born-again Christians. Particularly heavy emphasis was laid on the need for constant and knowledgeable use of the Bible in the counseling. Personal opinions and denominational biases were out! This emphasis on the Scriptures appealed to the assembly Christians, and their knowledge of the Bible soon became apparent. As a result, many more counselors and advisers were from the assembly than from any other local church. The local minister who was delegated to take charge of the inquiry room was a sound evangelical, well acquainted with assembly activities and Bible teaching. Before the Crusade opened, he came to me and said, "Brother Mac, you're more experienced in this biblical way of dealing with inquirers; give me your assistance in this important task." Naturally I was happy to do so, and night after night, with many brethren and sisters from the assembly, we dealt with anxious souls.

There were no Sunday morning or evening services at the Crusade, so we continued our normal schedule at Forest Avenue Tabernacle. Attendance was much larger than usual throughout the Crusade. Brother Harold Wildish was visiting at the assembly, and Billy Graham insisted I bring him to the platform of the Crusade tabernacle, where he introduced him to the 15,000 in attendance as "the preacher everyone in Jamaica knows." That night our Tabernacle was crowded to hear Brother Wildish.

The Bible preaching, punctuated by Billy's often-repeated "The Bible says . . . " created a most unusual interest in the Bible; hundreds of copies were purchased. Soon it became impossible to buy a Bible over the counter anywhere in Greensboro. The Greensboro Christians were in their element now. This great interest in the Bible, which continued after the Crusade closed, convinced me and the elders that we should capitalize on it and announce an evening Bible school. Because of my teaching association with Emmaus Bible School, I was able to secure courses and permission from the school to grade papers and issue certificates for completed courses. On Monday, December 10, 1951, the sessions began with 174 students registered for courses. Thirty-seven churches were represented from six denominations. In 1952, the enrollment reached 250. Three classes were held every Monday night, the courses including *What the Bible Teaches* (for which I had contributed a chapter), *Lessons in Christian Living,* and *Survey of the Old and New Testaments.* This meant three hours' teaching for me, after three (and sometimes four) services on the Lord's Day, plus a morning broadcast. But it was a happy time, and the fellowship was precious. Several even came into the assembly as a result.

The 1950's were the years of the "Baby Boom," the post-war surge in births. As a result, children became an increasingly important target for assembly outreach ministries. Not, indeed, that they had ever been unimportant! Because of our deep concern for the salvation of boys and girls, Lester Wilson and I had always incorporated special children's meetings into our gospel campaigns. These were a harbinger of a continuing care by the Greensboro assembly for the spiritual well-being of the young.

In 1944, prior to the Easter Conference at which he was to speak, A. P. Gibbs held one of his unique series for children at the Tabernacle. I recorded in a diary entry (expressing some amazement—and perhaps even slight envy!): "About 150 children present; brother Gibbs in complete control." Through the years, other gifted children's workers have held special services, greatly used by the Lord.

The faithful Sunday School staff are the real "infantry" of children's ministries. When we moved to Greensboro in 1943, a thriving Sunday School was already in progress. It soon entered a period of even greater growth, as the staff began to meet weekly for consultation on problems, methods, and teaching techniques. Concerned, however, about the need to go beyond the weekly 40 minutes with the children, the assembly began to explore other avenues of winning and guiding these young lives. In June of 1952, the Forest Avenue Tabernacle held its first Daily Vacation Bible School, under the leadership of Charles Williams, assisted by Edna Elmore (later Mrs. Bas Monnik), both of whom were home on vacation from the Emmaus Bible School in Chicago, where they were studying in preparation for the Lord's service. The attendance at this first

DVBS reached 86 on the closing day. Through the years this effort to reach the young has continued, with increasing interest, attendance, and blessing.

A more extended Christian environment for children was provided by summer camps, set up in cooperation with other Piedmont assemblies. Possibly it was my early experience as a Boy Scout troop leader before conversion that made me feel at home in a Christian camp. But how much more important and rewarding to teach boys and girls about the Saviour than about woodcraft lore and tying various kinds of knots! The first two-week camp was held in August of 1947 at a YMCA camp, Nawakwa, a few miles from Greensboro.

The accommodations were crude, to say the least! We had to truck in cots from the local YMCA each year, and if it rained the dirt road leading in to the camp would become so slippery and muddy the truck would mire up. There was one central community "outhouse" and shower. The swimming hole was extremely muddy. However, this unlikely spot was mightily used of the Lord to win hundreds of children and teens to the Lord.

In 1947, at that first camp, the first week for boys ("to chase the snakes out," as some chuckled later) was under the direction of Lester Wilson and Dick Andrews. Welcome Detweiler and I followed with a week of girls' camp, at which we had the great joy of seeing all the unsaved girls in camp (29 of them!) profess faith in the Lord. The convicting, converting power of the Spirit often continued far into the night, and cabin after cabin became the scene of tearful rejoicing as newborn converts and their companions sang praise to God. The first conversion in girls' camp that year was the younger sister of Edna Elmore. Edna later became the Greensboro assembly's first missionary to foreign lands.

This Piedmont Bible Camp continued for several years at Nawakwa, then for one year at a camp near Durham after the main building at Nawakwa burned to the ground, and for several years thereafter at the new Greensboro YMCA camp. All of these camps were vital, fruitful endeavors for children and teens. Many of us often thought how wonderful it would be to have campgrounds of our own, which would give us complete freedom of scheduling such outreaches for youth and adults as well. In 1959, the way to what seemed an impossible dream began to open up. A Christian in Winston Salem learned of a 75-acre tract of land on the north slope of Sauratown Mountain near Pinnacle, North Carolina, which was becoming available through some unusual circumstances.

In the spring of that year, Gertie and I, along with some other interested Christians, were invited to drive to the top of the mountain, where the WXII transmitting tower is located. From it we climbed down to this property. There we knelt, and I prayed that someday I would hear the voices of children singing praises to the Lord on this mountain. My prayer was answered in the summer of 1963 when the first week of camp was held at Mountain Top Youth Camp.

We have since been able to purchase an additional 25 acres, giving us a total campsite of 100 acres. Much prayer, persistence, hard work, and sacrificial giving have produced a beautiful camp with splendid facilities, able to accommodate weekly about 100 children and the requisite staff. Six weeks of camp for boys, girls, and teens are held each summer, followed by a Labor Day Weekend Retreat for college and career-age young adults. Over 100 Christians from area assemblies assist each year as counselors and staff. During most of the rest of the year, the camp is available to the area assemblies for special activities and weekend retreats, bringing in a total of approximately 2,500 youth and adults from over thirty area assemblies who use the camp annually. Our son Stan has had a long-standing burden for Mountain Top, serving as president of the Board of Directors from 1971-1989, when he left the business world to become fulltime Executive Director of the camp.

Keenly aware of the fact that Christian teens are the building material of future assemblies, the Forest Avenue Tabernacle focused from the beginning on developing a youth program that would, first, win them to Christ, then instruct them in the Scriptures, establish them in the truth, and instill in their hearts a desire to live for and serve the Lord. When we first moved to Greensboro, I began a Monday night gathering for assembly teens who met in the homes of various Christians for study of the Scofield Bible Course. Attendance at these averaged 25-30. Such youth meetings have continued ever since at Forest Avenue Tabernacle and later Shannon Hills Chapel in Greensboro. They have taken widely varied forms to meet the changing needs of the groups through the years, but the basic goals remain the same: to win souls and to provide fellowship, recreation, and ministry suited to teens. These youth groups have provided a continuing source of trained leaders to feed into the different assembly ministries.

We also saw the need for providing outlets for teens from the area assemblies to meet and fellowship with their peers. The first youth rally was held in Burlington in 1945, followed by others at more or less regular intervals. In 1961, an area-wide Youth Rally Committee was formed to plan and coordinate these rallies, eventually settling upon a semi-annual schedule. Attendance at the rallies varies from 200-300.

Sadly, in every generation, there are some children who are unable to profit fully from these Christ-based programs, because they live in areas and families where their basic needs cannot always be met. In the early 1950's, the Lord began burdening a young couple from the Augusta, Georgia, area to establish a home for such children. Gene and Sue Hollingsworth and their three children moved to Pittsboro, North Carolina, where a large, but run-down building had become available through the farsightedness of some North Carolina assembly businessmen, led by Reggie Edwards, Sr. of Fayetteville. With the enthusiastic support of the Piedmont assemblies, including our own, Gene and Sue were able to repair and paint the building and furnish it. In 1952, they opened the doors of the Pittsboro Christian Home for the first group of children. In my capacity as one of the Home's directors for many years, I saw firsthand the tremendous impact this work had on the lives of the children who passed through it. (Ed. note: W. E. (Gene) Hollingsworth has written an account of the Pittsboro Christian Home, which is now available.)

God's loving concern for families is manifested throughout the

Bible, as for example in Psalm 68, which speaks of Him as "a father of the fatherless" and as one who "setteth the solitary in families." Many of us who were coming into North Carolina in the 1940's had personally witnessed how summer Bible conferences in other parts of the country were able to strengthen both the individuals and the families who attended them. We felt the time had come to provide such a conference in the area to meet the needs of assembly families for an inexpensive and spiritually strengthening vacation. On October 23, 1944, Virgil Hollingsworth, William Bousfield, Lester Wilson, and I met at the YMCA owned conference grounds at Blue Ridge, near Black Mountain, North Carolina, and made arrangements to rent the facilities for a Bible conference the following year.

In July of 1945, the first Blue Ridge Summer Bible Conference was held, the convenors being Dick Andrews, Virgil Hollingsworth, James Innes, Lester Wilson, and I. The invited speakers were Harold Harper, Richard Hill, and Ernest Tatham. There were 270 present at the Lord's Supper. Added to the rich ministry and worship, the conference provided a full week of beautiful mountain scenery; hiking; pick-up games of softball, tennis, basketball, and volleyball; swimming in the lake (or for the daring, in a mountain spring-fed pond affectionately dubbed Eskimo Pool)); and for the more sedentary, there were the famed rocking chairs across the long front porch of Robert E. Lee Hall, where there was always a cool breeze and warm fellowship.

By 1957, changes in the policies for renting this conference ground brought about a move to the campus of Sullins College in Bristol, Virginia. After twenty fruitful years in Bristol, it moved to the Ben Lippen School in Asheville, and when a fire there destroyed the buildings, to Covenant College, atop Lookout Mountain in Chattanooga, Tennessee. As of this writing, the conference, now known as the Skyland Bible Conference, continues to meet there.

These conferences have done perhaps as much as any other assembly outreach to strengthen and refresh area Christians, by providing them with a week in an environment completely free of the world's interference, surrounded by every inducement to partake of the joy of Christian fellowship and service. Many have been saved at conference; many have been challenged to surrender their lives to the Lord or even to enter some specific avenue of Christian service. And new Christian homes have been established, as young adults met their future mates there. This became so common, in fact, that many fondly labeled the summer conference a "matchbox." I can attest to this as a definite fringe benefit, having met my own life's partner for the past nearly 60 years at just such a conference.

Not only did the Greensboro assembly thus take both leading and supporting roles in such area-wide ministries, but in the early 1950's, it sent one more branch "over the wall," this time to "the uttermost parts of the earth." Edna Elmore heard the gospel preached at the Forest Avenue Tabernacle in 1946 and came to our home at 622 Forest Street for counselling, where she received the Lord as personal Saviour. After completing her nurse's training in Augusta, Georgia, she returned to Greensboro, where she worked in the Wesley Long Hospital and was also active in the assembly. In 1951, she went to Emmaus for a year. During the following summer, she assisted in the first Daily Vacation Bible School, as previously mentioned. Although she had intended to return to Emmaus in the fall, I asked her to consider the many ways that she could serve in the local area. Consequently, she did stay on and was of invaluable assistance to me in grading the courses I taught following the Billy Graham Crusade. She also did much visitation and often did private-duty nursing for assembly Christians.

Edna had prayed for some time about the possibility of going to the mission field in Zaire, but after some contact with Dr. Stephens there and with Liddon Sheridan, she decided to wait on the Lord. At the Blue Ridge Conference in 1953, she met Edith Mieras, who spoke of the great need for Christian nurses in Africa. Her desire for this field of service renewed, Edna soon shared her exercise with the Greensboro elders. After prayer and consultation with her, they were happy to be able to write a commendation for North Carolina's first missionary to a foreign field! In June of 1954, she departed, with South Africa as her ultimate destination. After Edna's mar-

93

riage to Bas Monnik in 1958, the family, by then including young Stephen and David, came "home" to Greensboro on furlough in 1962. After getting to know Bas better, the Forest Avenue Tabernacle also commended him, before the Monniks returned to Mansfield Mission Station in South Africa.

For the next ten years after the recognition of elders in 1947, the Greensboro assembly continued to grow, not spectacularly but steadily, and with growth the responsibilities of the elders increased. Although they met regularly to discuss assembly matters, and these meetings lasted several hours, they found themselves increasingly occupied with material matters which could not be neglected. This seemed to parallel the situation recorded in Acts 6:1-2, which led the apostles to instruct the brethren to select "seven men of honest report, full of the Holy Ghost and wisdom, whom we may appoint over this business. But we will give ourselves continually to prayer and to the ministry of the Word" (vv. 3-4).

While these seven men are never specifically referred to as deacons, they certainly served in a special capacity in the church at Jerusalem. Later, when the Apostle Paul wrote to the church at Philippi, he addressed his epistle to "all the saints which are at Philippi with the bishops and deacons." There is a sense in which all the Christians are deacons (the word is literally *servants*), but the bishops (elders) and deacons at Philippi were definitely recognizable among the saints there. Inasmuch as the same passage which gives the qualifications for elders (1 Tim. 3) also gives those for deacons, it seems quite evident that there were those in the apostolic church who were set aside for special service in the assembly.

Based on this, the brethren met together at the Forest Avenue Tabernacle on May 1, 1957, and selected nine men to serve as deacons. It was decided that each should serve for a term of three years. From that time on, at the annual men's meeting, three brethren have been selected to replace the ones who had served their term. In this way there are always six experienced deacons serving with three new ones. This has proved most beneficial, resulting in the material matters of the assembly being attended to in an efficient manner, and also providing a large pool of brethren who are experienced in attending to assembly needs. Like the elders, the deacons meet regularly, a representative of the oversight being present to act as liaison between the two groups. The original nine deacons were John Ageon, Dale Andrews, L. W. Gerringer, John Goins, J. L. (Curly) Strickland, Paul Troxler, Charles Pauquette, E. L. (Chick) Whitley, and Dean Wrenn. Shortly after the election of the first deacons, a joint meeting of the elders and deacons was held for the purpose of prayerfully working out the responsibilities of each group in connection with assembly matters. This laid the foundation for the cooperative and coordinated functioning of the two groups which has continued to the present.

We rejoiced as we saw the Lord's work in Greensboro during these years. The fledgling assembly had left the nest and flown. Although we had our problems, as every group will, the Christians were united in their love for God's Word and His people.

During these years we also began to experience family changes, as our own fledglings began to try their wings. In 1952, Jack graduated from high school and enrolled at Elon College, a small liberal arts college near Burlington. After two years there, he joined the Army, stationed after basic training at Fort Stewart in Savannah, Georgia (more often referred to in mail home as "Swamp Stewart"!) Afterwards Jack returned home, but not for long. On November 3, 1956, I had the joy of performing the wedding for my oldest son, uniting Jack with Betty Coble, the daughter of one of our assembly elders. Jack soon returned to complete his education, majoring in accounting at the University of North Carolina at Chapel Hill.

Meanwhile Stan had finished high school in 1955, going on to North Carolina State University. The years from 1957 through 1959, when both sons graduated from their respective universities, were interesting, to say the least. Those who are acquainted with the intense athletic rivalry between the Tarheels and the Wolfpack will understand why!

Stan decided to fulfill his military obligation by enlisting in the National Guard for six years. After his six months of active duty, I was privileged to marry another son. On July 1, 1960, Stan was united in marriage with Helen Honeycutt, who had grown up under the ministry of Welcome Detweiler in the Durham Gospel Center.

Although Gertie and I rejoiced in our older sons' happy marriages, we were pleased not to have to face the empty nest quite yet. Ron was just entering senior high school. We didn't know it at the time, but we were about to enter the greatest personal test we had yet faced. Throughout it, this last son would be a particular comfort to both of us.

11
The Valley of the Shadow

"Yea, though I walk through the valley of the shadow of death, I will fear no evil, for Thou art with me" (Psalm 23:4).

The Christian life is one of hills and valleys; we ascend the steeps and descend into the shadows. In 1964, the Lord permitted me to be led into "the valley of the shadow of death" as I underwent serious brain surgery.

If the 1950's had brought us much to rejoice in, they had also brought us sorrow. Gertie's mother went to be with the Lord in 1950, followed by her father two years later. Then my own dear mother died in 1953. Dad was in very poor health at the time, so in November of that year we brought him to Greensboro. By December he was in the hospital with a heart condition and pneumonia.

In the spring, he was improved enough that we took him back to Galt, but within a month he was back in the hospital. Again we brought him to Greensboro, where for two years he was in and out of the hospital, Gertie and I having to care for him constantly. At the same time, Gertie's sister Georgie developed a malignancy, had surgery, and also had to be cared for in our home for a time.

The constant care of two invalids, added to family and assembly responsibilities, took its toll on both of us. Gertie became ill herself, and CMML generously arranged for her to go to Florida for a month's recuperation. Perhaps, then, it was not surprising when I started noticing a blacking out sensation, followed by extreme vertigo, when I would put my head back quickly in bed.

It was clear that we would have to place Dad in a retirement center where he could receive the nursing care he needed. We prayed much about this decision. We wanted to be sure that not only his physical, but also his spiritual needs would be met. The nearest assembly-operated home was in Longport, New Jersey. I remember praying, "Lord, let me someday see an assembly retirement center in North Carolina." The answer to that prayer did not come until many years later, and its story is for a later chapter. Meanwhile, we took Dad to Longport in September of 1955, where he remained until his homecall in 1963. Georgie had recovered sufficiently earlier to return to her home in Forest, Ontario.

Yet my symptoms showed no signs of alleviating even after we returned to our routine at home. It soon was evident that something had gone seriously amiss in my physical system—I was plagued by continual fatigue, nervousness, vertigo, severe headaches, loss of hearing in my left ear, partial paralysis in my left cheek and foot. Our family physician diagnosed the problem as severe stress and advised a period of complete rest. However, this brought only partial and temporary relief. Examinations by various specialists in Greensboro and elsewhere failed to produce a unanimous verdict as to the cause of the distressing symptoms. There were suggestions of a small brain tumor, but increasingly the inference was that my trouble was more psychosomatic than physical.

I felt that this could not be true. Being personally acquainted with a Christian psychiatrist in Cleveland, Ohio, I made an appointment with him. After a thorough examination, he said to me: "Harold, your problem is absolutely not psychosomatic; you have an acoustical tumor in the pons area of the brain. You must have it removed, or it will continue to grow and cause you to lose more and more control of your body. However, you need to know ahead of time that removing it will cause other problems. Even if the tumor is as small as a pea, it could not be removed by the most skilled neurosurgeon without some paralysis resulting."

Further tests and consultations in Greensboro led to the conclusion that I should enter hospital in Winston Salem for extensive tests at the Bowman Gray School of Medicine, one of the best research facilities in the southeastern United States. On June 7, 1964, I entered, and the next three days were filled with a strenuous routine of every type of test that seemed advisable. It was decided that Dr. Eban Alexander, an internationally-known neurosurgeon, would perform surgery on the 12th.

Dr. Alexander was completely honest with me and with the family. He made it clear that any surgery involving the brain was extremely risky. He explained how the location of the tumor meant that a major facial nerve would have to be severely stretched, perhaps even severed, causing partial or even total paralysis, and limited vision and hearing on the left side. He admitted that it was indeed possible that the surgery could leave me in a coma or unable to function normally for the rest of my life.

The prayers of the young Baptist chaplain meant much to all of us. He visited me the night before my surgery, and we discussed it together. He said, "I'm sure you are aware of the critical nature of the surgery tomorrow. How do you feel about it?"

"At perfect peace. It's in the Lord's hands, and so am I."

"That's fine, but a little unusual."

I explained, "Well, you see, brother, 38 years ago when I accepted Christ as my personal Saviour, I entered into peace with God. Three years later, I entered fulltime service for my Lord and have served Him for the past 35 years, preaching the gospel and teaching His Word. If I don't survive the surgery, and He is pleased to call me away, I will just be at home, absent from the body and present with the Lord. Not a bad prospect, is it? But I'll not be gone tomorrow; I'll be here. Drop around and visit me."

He asked me, "What gives you such confidence, Mr. Mackay?"

"The Bible. Since I began reading, studying, and preaching the Bible, it has become much more than a sacred book to me; it is God's personal message to me. In times of crisis, God usually impresses on my heart some specific portion of Scripture. My verse for tomorrow is John 11:4—'This sickness is not unto death, but for the glory of God.' That's my soft pillow for tonight." And I was indeed able to fall asleep that night, even without the sleeping pill.

By 8:30 the following morning, the pre-surgery tests began, and from 10:30 until 2:30 the surgery proceeded, guided by the omnipotent hand of the Great Physician. Dr. Alexander found a massive acoustical tumor adhering to the inside of the skull. He described it as "hard as a rock and large as a tennis ball." Removing it, as he had forewarned me, partially paralyzed my left side, left me deaf in my left ear, nearly blind in my left eye, and, although I didn't know it at the time, my face was badly distorted. The paralysis also meant that my left eyelid would not close normally; as a result, it had to be stitched partly closed, to avoid overexposure to light. This added to the disfigurement of my face.

By 10:00 PM, I was able to recognize Jack beside my bed and to speak to him, which was a great relief to all. Two days of severe pain were followed on the third day by a serious relapse, but two days later I was in a private room, cared for night and day by my faithful wife, our sons, and our daughters-in-law, as well as by the highly competent personnel of Bowman Gray.

This loving care undoubtedly led to my amazingly early release on June 29. Dr. Alexander and I both felt that I could recuperate better in our quiet home, surrounded by woods and fields, than in a hospital room. When I asked him about further therapy (for I had been learning to walk and move my left arm all over again), his reply was homespun common sense: "The best therapy in the world is doing things. Don't let anyone do for you what you can do for yourself; and what you can't do, don't be too proud to let someone do it for you." I have tried to live by that advice ever since.

And so, on a beautiful June day, Jack came to bring me home. He and Betty at that time had a new Rambler with a passenger seat that could recline. What a wonderful feeling to step out of that car, with the assistance of my waiting family, and feel the sun on my face again. And after nearly a month of hospital food, nothing in the world could have been any tastier than the hastily prepared meal of wieners, potatoes, and parsnips Gertie served me that night!

The den of our home was transformed into a sickroom, equipped with rented hospital bed. Gertie cared for me through the day, our sons taking over at night so she could sleep upstairs undisturbed. I was very weak and recovery was painfully slow. The month of July was one of tiny steps toward recovery, each one of such importance to me, to the family, and to the many who were supporting me in prayer at the assembly, that I kept a daily log of them for our encouragement. Some sample entries show typical experiences of those early days of convalescence: "July 5 (Sunday): Gertie out to the Lord's Supper; Jack stayed with me. July 6: Had several visitors. Jack Tuttle very gently gave me a haircut. July 7: Outdoors in the sunshine. Walked on lawn—wonderful! July 8: No sleeping pill last night. Shaved with safety razor." Until now Gertie had insisted I use the electric razor without a mirror, so that I would not see the terrible facial disfigurement. As I looked into that mirror on July 8, Satan whispered to me, "You'll never face an audience again!" Involuntarily I replied: "Thank you for the encouragement! My Lord designated you as a liar and the father of lies."

Perhaps this provoked my fighting spirit, but I redoubled my efforts at my own therapy: squeezing a rubber ball repeatedly, lying on the bed and performing bicycle movements with my legs, exercising my paralyzed vocal chords to try to regain control of my voice. The log entries soon sounded more encouraging, "July 15: At desk in the study 'puttering.' July 16: Driven by Ron to see Dr. Alexander. July 17: In the afternoon, left alone for the first time. July 20: Slept in upstairs bedroom for first time. July 24: Rented hospital equipment returned. July 25: Dressed in street clothes for first time."

From the month of August onward, there seemed to be increasing indications that I was on the way out of the Valley and slowly returning to a more normal lifestyle. On August 23, I attended the Lord's Supper for the first time in ten weeks. In October, the Lord graciously gave me the assurance that my days of service were not yet over. One evening there came a knock at our door. We opened it to admit Harold (Babe) Wilholt, a young man who had been attending the assembly. He had become deeply burdened about his need for salvation, so he drove out to discuss it with me. What a joy to be

101

able to counsel an anxious soul again! Babe Wilholt thus became the earnest of God's promise that there was still a time of service left to me.

On November 1, my log records that I attended all three services at the assembly that day for the first time since my surgery. That month I began taking treatments for the facial disfigurement from a local chiropractor. These were remarkably successful in eliminating the grotesquely twisted mouth and restoring a much more normal contour, thus making possible a resumption of my platform ministry. It understandably also had a most beneficial psychological effect on my recovery. As my physical strength slowly increased, I learned how to compensate for the loss of the balancing influence of the inner ear, which had been nullified by the surgery. This placed a much heavier burden on my legs and feet, greatly increasing my fatigue, but any tendency to self-pity was quickly erased by the sight of others on crutches and in wheelchairs.

By the beginning of 1966, I was able to resume a full schedule of services. During that year I preached 84 times, conducted 39 broadcasts, ministered at three conferences, and performed four wedding ceremonies, besides much visitation and counseling. Jim Redling had come in February of 1964, at the invitation of the Greensboro elders, to assist with the work at the Forest Avenue Tabernacle. This he did most commendably, both in the ministry and in visitation. In addition, his musical ability resulted in the formation of a choir, which added greatly to the services. In September of 1966, seeing that I was now able to resume most of my former preaching and pastoral work, Jim and Margaret located in Sanford to help the small assembly there.

Although I had been left with permanent disabilities after my surgery, the Lord graciously permitted my return to an active life of teaching, preaching, and writing. I knew that I could never again carry the workload of the past, which had at times included as many as twenty speaking engagements a week plus physical activities. But the Lord had, as He promised, been with me through the Valley, and He had led me back out into His fields of service.

12
Added Days

"Go, and say to Hezekiah, . . . behold, I will add unto thy days fifteen years" (Isa. 38:5).

When Hezekiah was "sick unto death," he prayed earnestly that the Lord might let him live. God, in His permissive will, granted this request, giving him an additional fifteen years. Hezekiah would have done far better to leave the matter in the Lord's hands; in his first official action after this reprieve, he managed to get his descendants into serious trouble with the Babylonians. Since the Lord has seen fit to spare me after my brush with death for considerably more than 15 years as of this writing, I pray daily that He will also permit me to live out my added days to His glory. In this final chapter, I would like to focus on a few key incidents in the years following my surgery: the Greensboro assembly's move from Forest Avenue Tabernacle to Shannon Hills, my privilege to "walk today where Jesus walked," and my shift from a spoken to a written ministry.

As the 1960's had brought about a turning point in my own life, so they brought major changes to the local assembly. Even though we had added a wing to the Tabernacle during the 1950's, giving much additional space, by 1962 we were again "full and running over," as the children's chorus says. After much discussion and prayer, we decided to hive off with a branch work. The mortgage to finance the addition to the Tabernacle was burned on October 11, 1962, so the assembly was in good financial condition to assist the beginning of a new work.

But where? The location of a new assembly would be a crucial aspect of its future growth and usefulness. First, a map was prepared showing the location of all the families in the fellowship. This seemed to point toward the southwestern part of the city as the most logical area to consider. A committee delegated to search for suitable property eventually located acreage on Vandalia Road, just off Interstate 85. On January 4, 1963, a tract of four acres was purchased from R. A. Gibbs, on the corner of West Vandalia and Rehobeth Church Roads. The full price of $10,000 was paid on January 23 from a building fund commenced earlier. One of the local Christians purchased an additional acre adjoining the property and held it for the assembly.

That the Lord had guided in selecting the site for the new chapel is abundantly clear from events that followed. It is near two interstate highways (85 and 40), and a main state highway (220) has since been rerouted very close to it. The neighborhood continues to grow, so that while there was one residential development nearby (Shannon Hills) at the time the chapel was erected, there are now six within easy reach.

As each step was taken in acquiring the property, the assembly as a whole was kept fully informed and a vote taken of all those in fellowship. Although the purpose had been to commence a branch work, as time passed there was a growing conviction that a building should be erected that would accommodate the entire assembly, and that the old Tabernacle should be sold. The neighborhood in which the Tabernacle was located was rapidly deteriorating; almost no young couples lived there, and parking space was very scarce. At a called meeting of the congregation on December 23, 1962, a large majority (124 to 5) voted in favor of moving the entire assembly to the new location on Vandalia Road. In May of 1963, a building committee was appointed to work with the architect on drawing up plans for the new building.

After receiving construction bids, we were able to determine that about $350,000 would be necessary to build and equip the new chapel. Although the number in fellowship in the assembly had increased through the years, it was not large by modern church standards, and all the Christians were definitely in the middle-class bracket. This sum thus presented a real challenge to faith. The Lord proved faithful, as He had in all the years since the commencement of the testimony. As plans began to materialize, interest in the building fund increased. By the end of 1966, it had reached over $80,000. With the sale of the Tabernacle expected to bring about $45,000, we secured a loan from Stewards Foundation for $220,000 (which was paid in full by May of 1979).

In the months that followed the groundbreaking on March 27, 1966, the Christians eagerly watched the progress of the construction. Various ones took the responsibility of furnishing different areas with the necessary items. A wonderful spirit of harmony and helpfulness was evident. When any particular skill was needed, it seemed to surface immediately among the men or women. It was a joyful time, truly reminiscent of the scenes described in Exodus 35-40, as the people of Israel built and furnished the tabernacle in the wilderness.

Eventually the building was completed, the furnishings and equipment installed, the final inspection made, the keys turned over to the trustees, and Shannon Hills Chapel had become a reality.

The first use of the new building was for a wedding I performed on June 3, 1967. The following day, about 300 gathered for the first Lord's Supper in the new building, and 626 were present for the Family Bible Hour at 11:00. I spoke on "The Shannon Hills Chapel—a Lighthouse, a Home, and a School—a Place of Light, Love, and Learning."

Because it was unusual in the assemblies to build such a large chapel, I wrote an explanation for the August 1967 issue of *Interest* magazine, "Why We Built Big in Greensboro." In it I gave seven reasons for our decision: because the Lord definitely led us to do so; because we needed the space for a growing work; because a large majority of the assembly Christians were in favor of doing so; to prove to the citizens of this city that scriptural principles are feasible in the twentieth century; that the city might have a strong fundamental testimony; that the assembly might be able to maintain a well-rounded program of activities for all ages; so there would be a strong home base from which future assemblies could branch out."

Because of our increasing size and an ever-widening program of activities during the 1960's, the elders again found that they were having to give undue amounts of time to material and programmatic activities. For example, we were having to line up arrangements for meals to be served at annual meetings, to arrange for flowers to be sent to the hospitalized, to be sure that bereaved families had a meal sent in. It occurred to me that a high percentage of such needs were those actually met by the women of the assembly; the problem was that the elders were having to make the arrangements and ask them to do these things. Why not have a committee of women who were delegated to plan and organize such activities?

On October 27, 1966, such a committee was elected by the ladies in fellowship at their annual meeting. Following the pattern that had proved so successful with the deacons, it is composed of nine members, each of whom serves for a term of three years. By this method, there are always six experienced sisters on the committee to guide the three newly-elected ones. The original nine were Judy Andrews, Nell Everhart, Nona Earnhardt, Lois Fitch, Gertrude Mackay, Helen Mackay, Hozelle Paris, Mildred Routh, and Carolyn Shelley.

With the move to Shannon Hills Chapel, a new phase of rapid growth occurred. Although the Lord had graciously enabled me to resume a near-normal schedule of activity during these years following my surgery, it became increasingly evident that I could not continue to meet all the needs that a full-time worker is called upon to meet. I expressed to the elders my desire to be relieved of some of the responsibilities I had carried so long.

After much prayer by all involved, it seemed to be clearly the Lord's will for J. Eddie Schwartz to locate in Greensboro. Saved in Richmond, Virginia, brother Schwartz had been commended to the work of the Lord by the assembly in that city and was laboring in Memphis, Tennessee. Accordingly, on the invitation of the Greensboro elders, in 1969 Eddie, his wife Louise, two daughters and a son, moved to Greensboro. Soon brother Schwartz found his days (and nights!) well filled with prayer and preparation, preaching and visitation, weddings and funerals, and sharing the radio broadcasts with me. Louise also became active in the Sunday School and sisters' activities. By then in my sixties, I greatly appreciated the resulting lighter load of responsibilities.

In 1972, while I was ministering at the Bristol Bible Conference, Gertie and I were offered a trip to Israel on a tour in December led by Clarence Low. We thankfully accepted the offer, even though I was still handicapped in walking by the lack of balance resulting from my 1964 brain surgery. Here was the opportunity to replace all the reading about Israel with the reality of visiting it!

And so on December 26, 1972, we boarded a plane and flew to New York, where we joined 23 other tour members, boarded an Air France Boeing 747 and crossed the Atlantic to Paris. Dinner was served on the plane at 8:15 PM, "Lights Out" at 9:30, "Lights On" at 12:00 midnight, and breakfast was served at 12:15 AM. A short night indeed for the 360 passengers aboard!

After a brief stop in Paris, we continued on to Tel Aviv. I shall never forget the thrill I experienced as the wheels of the plane touched the runway there. At Paris, there had been no exhilaration at the thought of being in the country of Bonaparte and Joan of Arc; nor had the later stop at Athens brought any recollection of the Grecian heroes of old or the famous philosophers of that land whom I had read often. But it was altogether different at Tel Aviv. At the first bump of the wheels on the tarmac, a great surge of emotion swelled through me. I was in the land of Joshua, of Gideon, of Saul and David and Jonathan, the land of Matthew, Joseph and Mary, and, above all, the land of my beloved Lord and Saviour, Jesus of Bethlehem, Nazareth, Jerusalem, and of Calvary. I was now to see the places of which I had preached so often, to stand at the Jordan, the Garden of Gethsemane, Calvary, the empty tomb, the Mount of Olives! It all seemed so familiar, for years had been spent in studying and speaking about these places and the events connected with them. It was 1:30 AM when we finally retired at Mount Scopus Hotel in Jerusalem, and rising time was 6:00 AM Another short

107

night! But what did it matter? One could sleep in America, but there would be so much to see in Israel.

On our first full day in Jerusalem, we saw many of the traditional sights, such as the Pool of Bethesda, Mount Moriah, the Temple area, and the Western (Wailing) Wall. However, the truly unforgettable event of the day was the visit to the garden tomb, followed by a celebration of the Lord's Supper there. How precious remembering the Lord can be when surrounded by the garden where He prayed, near the tomb which could not hold Him!

On our second day, we were off on the Jericho Road to visit Masada, which we reached after a brief stop at the traditional site of the Inn of the Good Samaritan. Masada deserves a much more detailed description than I can give here. It is a majestic escarpment on the southern end of the Judean desert, with a sheer drop of more than 1,300 feet to the western shore of the Dead Sea, about twenty miles from the site of ancient Sodom. In shape it has been likened to a gigantic stone battleship.

It gained fame mainly through the valiant stand of a garrison of Jewish patriots against the Roman conquerors under General Silva in 72 A.D. When their defenses had finally been breached and all hope of escape had dissipated, 360 men, women, and children died at their own hands rather than surrender to become slaves of their conquerors. Only two women, who had gone into hiding, remained alive to relate the moving tale.

During the final siege of Masada by the Roman legions, thousands of Jewish slaves were employed to build a massive ramp of earth and stones on which a siege tower with a huge battering ram was erected. On our visit, there was a cable car which transported us to the top of the ramp, but we were still far from the top. The engineers of the Israeli army who accompanied the archeological expedition in 1963 had constructed an ingenious stairway up the sheer face of the cliff. We were faced by a climb of eighty steps!

"Can you make it?" I was asked.

I replied, "I'll tell you when we get to the top."

And to the top I went, followed closely by my plucky wife. But even then there was more uphill travel. Eventually we reached the top, to be rewarded by a spectacular view of the Dead Sea, with the purple mountains of Moab in the distance, a view which took away what little breath we had left!

We toured the amazing excavated ruins, marveling at what we saw. But, "what goes up must come down (except prices and taxes!)" and while the trip down was not as strenuous as the climb up, it was not exactly a pleasant stroll. But it was well worth the effort; I consider Masada to be the most remarkable place I have ever visited. We traveled home that afternoon through Beersheba, Hebron, and Bethlehem.

The following days brought a whirlwind of other sightseeing, each place bringing back many memories of events recorded in God's Word. Daily I prepared devotionals for our group, based on some of these Bible stories whose scenes we were witnessing. One particularly memorable day we visited Galilee, where Christ spent His boyhood, called His disciples, and did His early preaching. As we crossed the Sea of Galilee, one of its characteristic sudden storms arose. I was at that moment preaching to the group on the incident recorded in Mark 4:36-41, when a storm arose as Jesus slept in the ship. The words He spoke when aroused by the frightened disciples, "Peace, be still," came to us all with the freshness of real experience. [Ed. note: Many years after this incident, when the Mackays were living at the Pittsboro Retirement Center, they received word of a man who had heard the recorded tape of this message and had received the Lord as his Saviour through it. They were thrilled to hear of this unknown fruit from their time in Israel.]

On our last day in Israel, we visited Acre, the ancient seaport on the Mediterranean, nine miles north of Haifa, which was captured by the Crusaders in the twelfth century. We toured the city, watching the patient coppersmiths ply their trade in their street shops. We bought one of their handmade plaques, of the spies with the grapes of Eschol, to adorn our living room wall as a reminder of our visit. The drive up Mount Carmel took us past the shrine of the B'hai cult, where the bones of the founder are entombed. From the top, we had a breathtaking view of the beautiful harbor below. Then we went on to Caesarea, where we climbed to the top of the restored Roman theater. Shechem was next, with a visit to Jacob's well. On our way back to Mount Scopus Hotel in Jerusalem, we saw Bethel in the distance. After a good dinner and a lively "sharing" meeting, we retired early in preparation for our 5:45 AM departure for Greece.

In Athens, we had good accommodations in the King Minas Hotel. An afternoon tour of the city took us to the Acropolis, the Parthenon, and Mars Hill, where the apostle Paul preached his famous sermon. After dusk, the beautiful Christmas lights illuminated the city, each street having lights of a different geometric design.

Ten of us visited the home of George Yphantides, an American missionary in that city, for a short meeting, highlighted by testimonies in Greek and English, the nearest to a "tongues" meeting I've participated in! It was my privilege to bring a message to the assembled company by interpretation. The following morning, George accompanied us on a brief trip to Corinth. Then it was back to our hotel in Athens to rest in preparation for our flight home.

When we touched down in Greensboro at 8:30 PM the following night, we were exhausted but exhilarated. I already knew, and would become even more aware in the months ahead, how much my own understanding of God's Word had been strengthened by actually seeing the places in which it is set. I longed to see my fellow-believers share that experience.

As 1978 drew near, bringing with it the 50th anniversary of my service for the Lord, I thought how wonderful it would be to take fifty local Christians on a "jubilee" tour to Israel. Two major questions arose: Who would lead the tour? What would be the response to the suggestion? One man, I felt, was best suited to be the tour leader: Ernest Woodhouse had led eight tours to Israel and was well acquainted with the country. He was an able Bible teacher and a most congenial brother. He and his wife would be ideal. I wrote to him, putting the proposition before him, and received a quick and affirmative response: he would be delighted. The announcement locally and in nearby North Carolina assemblies created an enthusiastic reception. A date was announced, registrations began to be received, and several preparatory meetings were arranged with brother Woodhouse. His experience proved to be invaluable in pre-tour planning and on the entire tour.

On Monday, November 6, 1978, a group of happy Christians boarded a SwissAir jumbo jet for our overseas flight, armed with a fifteen-page travelogue prepared by Joy Woodhouse. Ernie's expertise in using every available moment for profitable activity soon became apparent. It was a joy to Gertie and me to revisit many places seen on the tour five years earlier, as well as many new ones.

As the trip progressed, I had the growing feeling that something was distinguishing this visit from the first one. Gradually I realized what that difference was. On my first visit to the Holy Land, everything was so new that I was mainly occupied with the physical features of the places visited: "So this is Jerusalem? Jericho? Bethlehem?" But now, that initial novelty having receded, I was free to concentrate on the spiritual significance. Sometimes even the location suggested a spiritual lesson. For example, the well at Sychar, where Jesus offered the Samaritan woman the water of life, is located between Ebal and Gerizim, the mountains of cursing and of blessing respectively (Deut. 11:29, Jn. 4:1-15). Brother Woodhouse's reading of selected portions of Scripture at each place visited and his comments, based on his extensive Bible knowledge, were most appropriate and insightful.

The evening of Sunday, November 12, was spent at the Hassan Affendi al Arabi Restaurant as guests of Gabriel Khano, owner of the Guiding Star Travel Agency, the agency handling the tour arrangements. Mr. Khano conducted an interesting program in commemoration of my 50 years of service for the One whose earthly homeland we were now visiting. A moonlight bus ride to the mountaintop to view the lights of the city of the Great King concluded a memorable night for Gertie and me. The anniversary cake baked by the Khano family has long since disappeared, but the photo of the cake-cutting, now hanging on our den wall, is a constant reminder of a happy occasion.

111

Our homeward journey took us from the Ben Gurion Airport to Zurich, Switzerland, then on to Kennedy Airport in New York, and finally the last leg to Greensboro, where a welcoming party greeted our safe arrival after a wonderful, never-to-be-forgotten experience.

Many years ago, Dr. R. E. (Ed) Harlow, former missionary to Africa and first president of Emmaus Bible School, asked me: "Harold, how many persons, on an average, do you think you reach by each of your spoken messages?" Not having previously given the matter any serious thought, I could only venture a guess of two or three hundred, increased somewhat if recorded or broadcast.

His second question was, "Have you ever considered the fact that you could greatly increase that number by putting your teaching into print? It could then be circulated, reread, possibly translated into other languages, and preserved for future readers." This was thought-provoking and certainly deserved careful, prayerful consideration. I had, of course, at that time no inkling of the "valley experience" that lay ahead, but God did, and He was preparing me.

Through the years following that conversation, I occasionally published short pieces—magazine articles on Christian leadership or on Christ's coming, pamphlets such as *Christ the Gathering Center of His People, The Lord's Supper, Should Christian Women Wear a Headcovering?* and *Biblical Financial Principles.* In 1972, I wrote an Emmaus course, called *Countdown to Eternity,* on the dispensational interpretation of Scripture. I had also had a number of papers published from presentations I had made at various conferences. I never felt, however, that I had the time necessary for more extended writing.

During the late 1970's and the 1980's, as my continuing health problems forced me to relinquish more and more of my speaking and visitation, I began to pray further about writing as a productive avenue of service. My initial exercise was to put into print those church principles and practices which I had preached for many years, and which a careful study of Scripture had fully convinced me were the New Testament pattern for the Church. This I did, under the title *Assembly Distinctives,* published by Everyday Publications in 1981. Since then it has gone through at least five editions and has been translated into Spanish and French.

Since the night of my conversion on May 23, 1926, the foundation of my faith, the chart and compass of my life, and the sum and substance of my preaching has been the Word of God, the inspired infallible Bible. One of the burdens I have carried on my heart during my years of ministry has been that which Luke wrote to Theophilus, "That thou mightest know the certainty of those things wherein thou hast been instructed" (Lk. 1:4). Each rising generation of believers must be fully instructed in and thus become fully convinced of the absolute trustworthiness of the Bible. In an attempt to fulfill my responsibility in this crucial matter, I prepared a companion set of little books. The first, published by Walterick in 1985, was *The Story of Your Bible,* dealing with what the Bible contains, how it came to us, and why we can trust it. The second volume, *The Study of Your Bible,* published by Walterick in 1988, sought to encourage readers *about* the Bible to become students *of* it. The suggestions I made in this little book are the fruit of my personal study for over sixty years.

My last published book, *The Coming of Christ* (Walterick, 1989), discusses the Rapture as distinguished from the Revelation, pre- and post-Tribulation views, and the literal millennial kingdom. I also currently have several unpublished manuscripts: "Back to Bible Basics," "Biblical Dispensationalism," "Marriage, Divorce, and Remarriage," and "The Changeless Christ."

As my life draws toward its close, I find myself longing with heightened anticipation for the return of my Lord. Today moral and spiritual darkness deepens in the world: "Evil men and seducers wax worse and worse, deceiving and being deceived" (2 Tim. 3:13). False cults flourish like noxious weeds, poisoning the minds of deluded followers. Man's impiety and impurity continue to gnaw away at the very vitals of civilization like a malignant cancer, while the professing church turns its back on the inspired Bible and closes its doors to Christ. But the Christian has a blessed hope—the coming of the "Bright and Morning Star."

Many years ago, somewhere in my reading, I came across the account of an incident in the life of a well-known Bible teacher which I have always felt concisely and correctly illustrates the sequence of events connected with the Lord's coming *for* His people in the Rapture and His later post-Tribulation coming *with* them to set up the millennial kingdom. This servant of Christ was traveling by train to fill an engagement. He could hear a storm raging outside in the night. Peering out the window of his Pullman compartment, he could see nothing in the prevailing darkness, until suddenly the clouds parted and the bright beams of the morning star shone through the gloom. But only for a moment! Then the clouds closed in once again, and the storm continued with even greater intensity. Lying back upon his bed, he waited until the rising sun heralded a new, fresh day.

So it will be with the Church. After the appearance of Christ— the Morning Star in the heavens—when His people rise to meet Him, the storm clouds will close in once again over this doomed world, darker and more devastating than ever, as apocalyptic judgments precede the coming of the Lord with His saints and angels: "Immediately after the tribulation of those days . . . they shall see the Son of man coming in the clouds of heaven with power and great glory" (Mt. 24:29-30).

Meanwhile, we can only wait and hope. It has been well said, "For the Christian, the future is as bright as the promises of God." And the promises concerning Christ's coming certainly illuminate the future of the believer with the bright rays of an eternal hope.

One thing that I have been promised is a perfect replacement for this worn-out physical body. It is said that John Quincy Adams was taking his morning walk on one occasion when he was accosted by a passerby, "How is John Quincy Adams this morning?"

He replied, "John Quincy Adams is fine, thank you, although the house he resides in is in constant need of repairs." Now in my eighties, I can echo his sentiments, but I have been promised, not repairs, but a permanent replacement: "This corruptible must put on incorruption, and this mortal must put on immortality" (1 Cor. 15:53).

As I await the return of my Lord, I must not simply yearn for the fulfillment of those promises, however; I must remain active. In my eighties, the lack of physical stamina makes impossible those long itineraries of the past, during which I engaged in evangelistic and expository ministry in many places. Facial pain and paralysis make it impossible to give even a short message, but there is still much that can be done, with some necessary adjustment in our lifestyle and activities. The promise is: "They shall still bring forth fruit in old age" (Ps. 92:14). Now that my physical strength and faculties are failing, though, I am thankful to be able to say in all honesty and humility that I sought in earlier years to use unreservedly for the Lord the strength and ability I possessed.

I conclude these reflections with a slightly altered rendering of words written by Cleaver, a dedicated messenger of the Cross to the Muslims:

> When life here is ended, how glad I shall be
> That the best of my life has been yielded to Thee.
> I shall not regret one mite that I gave
> Of labor or time one sinner to save.
> The pathway at times may have seemed to be rough,
> But Thy goodness and guidance was more than enough.
> When life here is over, how glad I shall be
> That the life Thou didst give me was giv'n back to Thee.

Co-Author's Afterword

On a sunny Sunday morning in April, at approximately ten o'clock, worship was ascending from assembled believers all over the eastern part of the country. Small and large groups gathered reverently around the simple symbols of bread and wine, honoring the One who had said, "This do in remembrance of Me." After an unusually cold and rainy spring in North Carolina, dogwoods and apple trees splashed their early whiteness against the green finally visible across fields and forests. In the eternal cycle of the seasons, life was again overcoming death; in the eternal mystery of the Remembrance Feast, men and women wondered afresh at the death that gave them life.

A Presence, unseen by others, approached a frail form in a hospital bed and whispered quietly into his ear, "Well done, thou good and faithful servant. Enter thou into the joy of thy Lord." At the long-awaited beckoning, Harold G. Mackay arose eagerly from that form and ascended, with the rising worship, into the presence of his Saviour. A nurse, feeling for a pulse, shook her head and walked to the telephone.

On Wednesday, April 21, following a funeral service at Shannon Hills Chapel, Dad's mortal remains were laid to rest in a quiet corner of a cemetery in Greensboro, near their home of 40 years. The day had been rainy, but the sun broke through the clouds, as a quiet group of friends and family gathered around the casket covered with the roses Dad had so loved in life. Charles Crawford and Dick Andrews read the beautiful promises of the resurrection from God's Word: "So, when this corruptible shall have put on incorruption, and this mortal shall have put on immortality, then shall be brought to pass the saying that is written, Death is swallowed up in victory. O death, where is thy sting? O grave, where is thy victory?"

As of this writing in June of 1993, Mom is living at the Pittsboro Christian Village retirement center. Many other friends that she and Dad developed during their years of service together are there also, so that she has happy fellowship with them at meals, during the daily special activities, and as people drop by her room to visit. The assembly chapel is connected by a hallway to the building, so that it is easy for her to get to the meetings when she is able to do so.

The family has grown into quite a clan! In addition to Jack and Stan's marriages, mentioned in Chapter 10, Ron later married the former June Hughes. They have five children—Andrea, Bruce, Todd, Heather, and Joshua, and now five grandchildren from the three oldest. Jack and Betty's son, Mike, completed law school this spring. Stan and Helen's son, Kerry, the first Mackay grandchild, and their daughter, Lauren, are both married and have presented the Mackays with three little great-granddaughters. On November 25, 1991, the family honored Mom and Dad with a sixtieth wedding anniversary reception, at which they had a family picture made. Two of the great-grandchildren were born after this picture.

The Mackays were able to remain in their home on Vandalia Road in Greensboro through February of 1992, with much assistance from family and friends, but it had become apparent, because of their frequent falls and other health problems, that they needed around-the-clock care. Dad's prayer that he would someday see an assembly retirement center in North Carolina had come true. Because of increasing government regulation of children's homes and the growth of the state supported foster home plan for children who needed temporary care, the Pittsboro Christian Home phased out. After much prayer, the directors decided to convert the property into a retirement community, consisting of individual homes, apartments or rooms in the main building, and limited nursing care capability. In 1975, the Pittsboro Christian Home (later renamed Pittsboro Christian Village) re-opened its doors, this time to meet the needs of the assemblies' retirees.

When the day came that we as a family had to make the painful decision that Dad and Mom had had to make about his father in 1955, it was a comfort to have available this beautiful home with twenty-four-hour nursing care and an adjoining chapel. It is only a 45-minute drive from our homes in Greensboro. On March 2, 1992, the Mackays moved into an airy, attractive room, already decorated with the family pictures and Scripture text plaques they had chosen to take. Such transitions in life are never easy, but with the Lord's help, this one was as smooth and comfortable as possible.

It was also a blessing that they were already settled there and that trained and caring people surrounded them on March 6, 1993, when Dad fell in the dining room, breaking a hip. During the six weeks that followed, although he put up quite a fight, he finally succumbed to the ensuing complications.

During the last days, when it had become apparent the end was near, Stan got out a sheet of suggestions for the funeral that Dad had typed seven years before, almost to the day. On the back of this sheet, Dad had typed a fragment of remembered poetry by John Oxenham:

> *Lord, when Thou seest that my work on earth is done,*
> *Let me not linger on*
> *With failing powers*
> *Adown the weary hours,*
> *A workless worker in a world of work.*
> *But, with a word, just bid me home,*
> *And I will come, right gladly,*
> *Yea, right gladly will I come.*